Cactus Country

AN ILLUSTRATED GUIDE

JOHN A. MURRAY

Photographs by John A. Murray

ROBERTS RINEHART PUBLISHERS

BOULDER, COLORADO

International Standard Book Number 1-57098-076-4
Library of Congress Catalog Card Number 96-67081

Published by Roberts Rinehart Publishers
5455 Spine Road
Boulder, Colorado 80301

Published in the UK and Ireland by
Roberts Rinehart Publishers
Trinity House, Charleston Road
Dublin 6, Ireland

Distributed in the U.S. and Canada by Publishers Group West

Printed in Hong Kong

For my son, Naoki

Contents

Deserts of the American Southwest

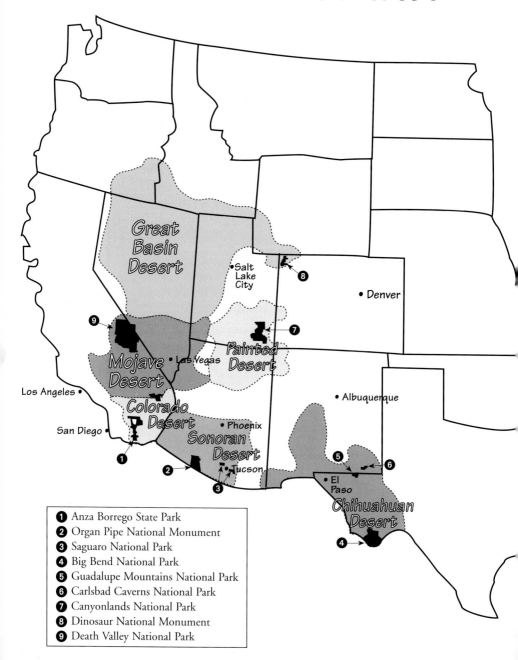

1. Anza Borrego State Park
2. Organ Pipe National Monument
3. Saguaro National Park
4. Big Bend National Park
5. Guadalupe Mountains National Park
6. Carlsbad Caverns National Park
7. Canyonlands National Park
8. Dinosaur National Monument
9. Death Valley National Park

DOCTOR JOHNSON, who occasionally went into the country to see his friends, but never to see the country, who thought a man demented who enjoyed living out of town; and who cared for a tree only as firewood or lumber, what would he have had to say about the desert and its confines? In his classic time, and in all the long time before him, the earth and the beauty therof remained comparatively unnoticed and unknown. Scott, Byron, Hugo,— not one of the old romanticists ever knew Nature except as in some strained way symbolic of human happiness or misery. . . . But the Nature-lover of the present, who has taken so kindly to the minor beauties of the world, has perhaps a wider horizon than his predecessors. Not that his positive knowledge is so much greater, but rather where he lacks in knowledge he declines to condemn. He knows that Nature did not give all her energy to the large things and all her weaknesses to the small things; he knows now that she works by law and labors alike for all; he knows now that back of everything is a purpose, and if he can discover the purpose he cannot choose but admire the product. . . . Nature never intended that we should fully understand. That we have stumbled upon some knowledge of her laws was more accident than design. We have by some strange chance groped our way to the Gate of the Garden, and there we stand, staring through the closed bars, with the wonder of little children. Alas! we shall always grope! And shall we ever cease to wonder?

— John C. Van Dyke
from *The Desert*

Preface

This is a place far, far from the tumult of mar-
kets, streets and courthouses. Here I drink deep
of the solitude of the universe. There is no
sound except the soft music made by the wind
blowing through the bunch grass.
—William O. Douglas, "Baboquivari"
from *My Wilderness*

DESERTS. There are deserts in the middle of crowded cities. You see them
in the vacant eyes of people living without love, without faith, without opportunity, estranged from nature and themselves. There are deserts on Mars, I am
told, that put Death Valley to shame. There are deserts in the future where
there are forests today. There are forests today where there were once deserts.
There are deserts at the bottom of the sea and there are deserts on the tops of
mountains. There are deserts with no heat, as on Antarctica, and deserts with
no air, as on the moon. Some historians refer to the European Middle Ages as
a desert. To a carpenter ant, the rooftop of your home is a desert. When I
think of my life, I think of times that have been deserts.

This is not a book about those kinds of deserts, although interesting
books could be written about each. *Cactus Country* is devoted to the six
desert provinces of western North America: Mojave, Colorado (a region of
the Sonoran), Sonoran, Chihuahuan, Great Basin, and Painted (a region of
the Great Basin). Together, these six deserts comprise over half-a-million
square miles. In total size they rank fifth among the deserts of the world.
Although all deserts on the planet have one feature in common — aridity —
they are quite varied in terms of fauna and flora, physiographic features, and
human adaptations. This guide is a celebration and exploration of the

American deserts, which harbor such diverse lifeforms as bighorns and burros, spadefoot toads and saguaro cactus, Jerusalem crickets and Joshua trees, pup fish and prospectors. It is not meant to be comprehensive — many more pages would be required to do that — but is, rather, selective, providing general advice, suggesting side trips, warning of hazards, noting history both human and natural, pointing out landmarks, indicating routes.

To some the desert is the "big nowhere," a sun-washed solitude of mirages and shifting sands, a rocky wasteland to speed through with plenty of water and preferably under the stars. To others it is a sanctuary to seek out, a serene landscape with the austere features of eternity, a quiet realm where life finds relief and renewal. This book is for the latter. In the crowded decades that will follow our own, these desert places will no doubt become increasingly important. In recognition of this fact, the United States Congress in 1994 passed into law the California Desert Protection Act. This historic legislation gave full wilderness protection to millions of acres of desert in Southern California. Over 70 separate wilderness areas, primarily on BLM land, were established. The bill also created the Mojave National Preserve, Joshua Tree National Park and Death Valley National Park. At 3.3 million acres, Death Valley is now the largest national park outside of Alaska. In addition to creating these new federal conservation units, the Desert Protection Act refocused national attention and discourse on the importance of deserts to our way of life, both as ecosystems rich in biota and as an intrinsic part of our frontier heritage.

We are a people whose character was quarried from the rock of travail, forged in the crucible of change, and refined among the elements of risk and chance. In these remote wild areas, posterity will forever be able to experience the adversity and danger that was so much a part of forming the distinctive American spirit. It was that same daring and determination, a quarter of a century ago, that put Americans on the trackless deserts of the moon, and summons the next generation to explore the distant red deserts of Mars. In the desert places of western North America, our children and their children will forever be able to enter a time machine and walk the same rough trails of the frontier pioneers. The value of this opportunity cannot be overestimated.

People sometimes forget that one of the formative experiences in the early years of our first president was his survey of the upper Ohio Valley, at the time a *terra incognita* beyond the mountains of western Virginia. Similarly, when young Theodore Roosevelt arrived in the Dakota Territory in 1883, it was still a rugged wilderness inhabited by grizzlies and wolves. These experiences prepared both men for active, strenuous lives that would one day be immortalized in the rock of Mount Rushmore. To my way of thinking, we preserve these desert places not only for their aesthetic and scientific value, but also for their ability to build character in our young people. So long as they remain intact, our freedom and independence will be kept alive. The wilderness they preserve is as much a part of the American way of life as any word in the Constitution.

Come with me now as we explore the sand dunes and salt playas, barrancas and bajadas, arroyos and oases of what is called, for lack of a better word, the desert. It is a region deceptive in simplicity, diverse in possibilities, dazzling in beauty. The root word of desert is the Latin *desertus,* meaning "abandoned." The desert is a place to abandon all that is unimportant and embrace a larger, richer world. For the dry lands are not a sterile waste incapable of supporting life, but rather a fertile paradise full of plants and animals, myths and legends, histories and chronicles, mysteries and secrets. In time you may come to agree with that well-known desert aficionado Edward Abbey, who once wrote that "In my case it was love at first sight. This desert, all deserts, any desert."

Acknowledgments

I have many to thank. To Jeff Gnasse, a fellow desert lover and landscape photographer *par excellence*, I must express gratitude for friendship, guidance and inspiration. Thanks also to naturalist/photographer Rick McIntyre, who has been helpful in so many ways over the years. Various officials at the following federal offices were immensely helpful with this project: Big Bend National Park, Bureau of Land Management, Cabeza Prieta National Wildlife Refuge, Death Valley National Park, Great Basin National Park, Organ Pipe National Monument, Saguaro National Park, U.S. Fish and Wildlife Service, Endangered Species Office (Region 2), White Sands National Monument. Employees at the Western History Collection of the Denver Public Library, and the Photo Library of the United States Geographic Survey, Denver Federal Center, were also helpful in securing archival images. Finally, I must thank publisher Rick Rinehart for enthusiastically supporting this project from the beginning.

Teddy bear cholla, Joshua Tree National Park, California (Mojave Desert)

Introduction

When I go back, as I must, to live in a world
almost wholly man-made and almost wholly
absorbed in problems which man himself has
created, I shall often return in memory to things
seen and done during my desert interlude...I
shall not forget its lesson: much can be lacking
in the middle of plenty; on the other hand,
where some things are scarce others, no less
desirable, may abound.

— Joseph Wood Krutch,
The Desert Year

THE FIRST TIME I SAW A DESERT was twenty years ago. A different time, a
similar time. Some would say a fairer time. Others would not wish to visit
that decade again. In any event, the introduction occurred in early August.
Most of the country was enjoying the best days of summer — bicycling the
boardwalk at Ocean City or munching a bag of popcorn behind home plate
at Riverfront Stadium. Touring the new exhibit at the art museum or
watching a romantic matinee. Fattening steers for the Iowa State Fair or
steering canoes to the far end of a Minnesota lake. In the Tetons, the
coureur du bois were shivering in mummy bags each morning, waiting for
the sun to clear Two Ocean Plateau and warm the high timbered valleys.
Not so for the members of a certain Marine air-base squadron. Our distant
uncle had arranged for us to spend a month in the Mojave, at a sunny little
place in the middle of nowhere. A forlorn forgotten valley as flat as it was
empty. Here a small expeditionary runway was located, and around it we
toiled like roadies at a rock concert. First task each morning was to shake

the scorpions and sidewinders from our boots. The sidewinders were tiny harmless-looking snakes, but the sergeant major claimed their venom would cause human flesh to putrefy from the bone. So we treated the handsome buzzing serpents with respect. Pushed them gently out of the tents with rifle muzzles and let them slither away unmolested through the creosote. Bad luck to kill a snake, especially in its home. The scorpions we squashed. Couldn't help it. Simple reflex. The most diabolical creature ever conjured up from DNA. Then we hiked over to the shaded water buffalo (water tank), thoroughly drenched white towels and tenderly placed them inside our steel helmets. There they remained like Arabian burnooses, periodically remoistened, for the duration of the day. In this way we kept what remained of our brains from cooking.

Normally the air temperature reached the neighborhood of 100 degrees shortly after breakfast. Then it proceeded to become hotter. And hotter. Until finally it became unbelievably hot. Temperatures as high as 114 degrees were duly noted and grimly joked about. Curious ravens, alighting on the metal runway panels, immediately flapped off, their feet scorched. At such times you dream of water as a boiler's mate six months on the Indian Ocean dreams of a bar in Manila, as a Congressman squirming at a press conference yearns for a lobbyist to explain his own bill to him, as a scholar in an airport newstand hallucinates a volume of Elizabethan poetry.

One day we noticed a peculiar line of black clouds building to the southwest. Fifteen minutes later our tents were swept from the earth in a sand storm from the Book of Isaiah. Then came the rain. But this was not rain. It was a biblical effusion, a drenching bottomless deluge, a thundering waterfall that would, if unchecked, soon flood iniquity from that province of the world. Somewhere in the atmosphere above, a black anvil cloud was climbing toward outer space. Down the center of that column poured the heavens. Never in North America had I seen such a violent monsoon. Eventually the dark colossus rolled east toward Nevada. In its wake the floor of the desert, like a poorly drained parking lot, was covered with several inches of water. An hour after the tempest was over the last drop of water had evaporated back into the sky from which it had been hurled. Our helicopters were turned into expensive pieces of junk, with sand driven into all their private places. The jets, on loan from an aircraft carrier, had fortunately been ordered into the air moments before the typhoon struck. Only the command post remained — a sturdy geodesic dome containing a soon-to-be general and his various attendants.

And still the sun bore down upon us. A humorless relentless piece of burning phosphorus slowly inching its way across a chromium blue sky. The ancient god of the Egyptians, Phoenicians, Greeks, Etruscans, Romans, Saxons, and Druids. A gigantic fusion bomb that will take ten billion years to fully explode. The beginning and the end of it all. Several men were lucky. Suffering heat exhaustion, they were evacuated to the air-conditioned infirmary at mainside where they could eat ice cream and discuss the future of the Republican Party with the Navy nurses. The rest of us were stuck like ants inside a self-cleaning oven until our "training cycle" was completed.

A few of us returned from that experience with a strange, some might say morbid, affection for the dry dessicated lands. The beauty of the landscape, especially just before sunrise, impoverishes the pen of one so unskilled as myself. Let us just say that an otherwordly radiance gradually makes its presence known in the east. The wrinkled, stark mountains assume fantastic colors. Canyons emerge from the shadows. Peaks sharpen themselves against a hard blue sky. A distant cloud turns red as an ocotillo blossom, a deer's heart, a ruby hit by a laser. The last somewhat mild breeze of night stirs. No sounds, no birds, no crickets even, because, remember, this is the Mojave desert in the summer. And then there is a sudden blinding nuclear flash and another dutiful tour in the inferno begins. But for those few brief moments — a sprinkling of stars to the west, a luminous miracle about to occur in the east — the desert, even in August, is pure revelation.

II

That is a word picture of the desert I personally love the most, the Mojave. But what *is* a desert, in the dispassionate, scientific sense? How to define it, classify it, abstractly describe it? Geographers say that a desert is a place with an average of ten or fewer inches of rainfall annually. Sometimes the precipitation is much less, as was the case from October 3, 1912 to November 8, 1914 in Bagdad, California, where it did not rain once in 767 days. Other times it is more, but never much more. They further surprise, even alarm us by stating that between one-fifth and one-third of Earth's land surface is desert (the exact proportion subject to debate). And that the deserts are collectively growing in size each year. Most of the deserts, as it turns out, are found between the Tropic of Cancer and the Tropic of Capricorn — a result of global wind patterns that, in turn, are caused by the complicated physics of a rotating sphere. The bulk of the deserts are located in far-away places: North Africa, the Middle East, Central Asia, and, of course, Australia (an aboriginal dream-time desert fringed with topless beaches).

The scientific people have invented names for all kinds of deserts: trade wind deserts, midlatitude deserts, rain shadow deserts, coastal deserts, monsoon deserts, polar deserts, paleodeserts, and extraterrestrial deserts. In the United States we have no extraterrestrial deserts (though several vice presidents reputedly have had them between their ears), but we do have midlatitude (Organ Pipe National Monument), rain shadow (Joshua Tree National Park), and paleodeserts (Nebraska sand hills). Elsewhere, there are equally striking examples of various desert types, as in the Turpan Depression of China's Tian Shan Mountains (rain shadow), or in the endless dunes of Africa's Sahara (trade wind), or in the parched, empty quarters of Namibia's Skeleton Coast (coastal desert). The dry valleys of Antarctica's uncharted inner mountains have been ice-free polar deserts for thousands of years, with snow dunes scattered here and there in frozen imitation of sand dunes. Along the Thar Desert of the Indus River floodplain, we have a monsoon desert with single dunes that stretch for miles. On Mars we have a world that, outside of the poles, is completely a desert. At certain times the whole red planet is enveloped in sand storms. One can only speculate as to how Mars lost its atmosphere and water, but the image of it hanging there, totally dead among the twinkling stars, serves to many as a powerful example.

Sand is by no means synonymous with deserts. In fact, 80 percent of deserts are characterized by other features: loose gravel, hard pavements, rock outcroppings, talus slides, uneroded uplands, alkaline flats, fossil riverbeds, dry arroyos and washes, bolsons (vast basins), playas (dead lakes), bajadas (alluvial fans), crystalline mountains. Fully half of all desert surfaces are comprised of loose gravels and occasional cobble. But sand is for some reason always associated with deserts. Winds — eolian processes — are primarily responsible for moving desert sand as they erode, transport and deposit minute ground-up specks of the Earth's mantle. Given sufficient time and favorable circumstances, the winds sculpt sand into lovely formations known as dunes, of which there are five types: crescent, linear, star, dome, and parabolic. The first is the one you are most likely to see, and the third, a radially symmetric dune formed by crosswinds, is the rarest. Parabolic dunes are the largest. The longest known parabolic dune had a ridge five miles long. Sometimes nature complicates matters for us by mixing various dune types together. In that way, she keeps the scientists guessing and the nature writers honest.

We come now to plants, and their strategies for survival in the desert. Insofar as the journey of human life can often be compared to crossing a desert, the lessons are not entirely academic. Use whatever metaphor for

California fan palm oasis, Anza Borrego State Park, California (Colorado Desert)

Sonoran desert vegetation, Organ Pipe National Monument, Arizona

water you wish — love, money, time. In each case, the desert plants have something, figuratively speaking, to teach us. The most important fact that desert plants have to contend with is the scarcity of water. I suppose in many cases, scarcity is a laughable understatement. When water finally arrives — often at unpredictable intervals — it must be both hoarded and protected like so much gold dust in a prospector's glass vial. Once water is secured, plants can move toward their primary objective, the goal of every organism, which is reproduction. But first things first. To obtain water, plants sometimes send their roots deeply into and widely across the earth. Often these roots must be tolerant of soils with high alkalinity or salt content. Walking a deep arroyo in the Sonoran Desert, I once saw exposed mesquite roots that extended fifteen feet into the ground. Three quarters of the mature plant was underground, with only a small quantity of branches and leaves exposed to the sun. In the desert, more so than in forests or woodlands, quite a bit of the biomass is below ground.

Some plants cannot contend with drought. When it becomes extremely dry, they simply die. But these ephemerals leave seeds behind that can sprout when conditions (substantial rainfall) are more favorable. Other plants — species such as ocotillo, saguaro cactus, creosote — are more drought tolerant, and have adapted fascinating strategies for survival. The creosote, for example, releases a chemical through its roots that inhibits the growth of other creosote plants. Thus, when you are driving through Death Valley and look out at a creosote-covered flat, you notice that the plants are uniformly spaced. It's almost as if a gardener came through and planted each one with a tape measure stretched radially from the nearest plants. In this way, each creosote receives enough water. We might say this is a cooperative strategy that enables the resident organisms to collectively inhabit a large area without conflict. The ultimate democracy — to each according to its need.

Saguaro cactus, by contrast, store water in well-protected inner tissue. The outside of the plant presents a thick, glossy surface that reflects the light of the sun and decreases water loss. Further, its razor-sharp spines discourage animals from stealing the water, as well as refract light. Also, the saguaro cactus opens its stomates — leaf or stem pores — briefly at night, rather than during the day when it would risk evaporative loss. The stomates must be opened regularly in order to discharge and absorb various gases that are part of the photosynthetic process. Another common desert plant that deals with heat and drought successfully is the ocotillo (which looks like a tarantula turned over on its back). The ocotillo grows leaves only on its long spiny stalks for a measured interval after a good rain. For the rest of the year, the stalks bear no leaves, thus reducing the possibility of water loss. Like the saguaro, the ocotillo also spreads its roots in a wide, shallow arc, maximizing the chances to absorb water.

Desert animals face the same challenge as plants in terms of heat and aridity. They have one significant advantage over plants, though, and that is that they can move around — on legs, wings, or, in the case of snakes, through muscular body motion. The most common technique for dealing with the unpleasant situation above ground is to retire to a den below ground. Day hikers in the desert often comment that the landscape appears to be devoid of animal life. Actually, there are animals everywhere. They are just smart enough be out of the heat. Once the stars appear they venture forth — elf owls, rosy boas, kit foxes, white-tail deer, ghost-faced bats. Desert animals also exhibit migratory patterns, moving higher or lower seasonally to adjust to plant resources. Thus we see deer, for example, summering at the higher elevations and wintering in lower deserts. Birds also take advantage of the mild desert winters, returning each autumn from snowed-in areas far to the north.

One of the most fascinating groups of desert animals are the pupfish. These are, without a doubt, the toughest fish in the world. Imagine living in a salty pond five times saltier than seawater, in which the temperature regularly surpasses 110 degrees Fahrenheit, with oxygen levels one-fiftieth of what is normally required for fish to live. These durable animals have the stoic constitutions of the early Christians, with no one to memorialize their heroic efforts but a few inarticulate nature writers. Equally amazing are kangaroo rats, which can live and die without ever tasting a drop of water. How so? With a metabolism that can magically extract water from food, and by carefully plugging its burrow opening, like a vampire, every dawn so that it may escape the ruinous rays of the sun. The kangaroo rat, and this is disgusting, also consumes its own fecal pellets to obtain vitamins and additional water.

The desert tortoise is another one of my favorites. Unlike the kangaroo rat, the desert tortoise must have water now and then. When it does drink, the armor-plated reptile can nearly double its body weight. This water is ultimately stored in, of all places, the bladder. The tortoise has a strategy for dealing with the aridity similar to that of the grizzly bear and the cold — when temperatures and lack of food become too much for it to deal with, the tortoise crawls into a deep burrow and takes a long, four-to-five-month nap.

The desert bighorn sheep, by contrast, cannot dig a burrow. It must endure the interminable bitter stretches of heat above ground. And the bighorn also must deal with predators — mountain lions, coyotes, human hunters. To avoid its enemies, the sheep live for the most part in or near the most rocky, desolate desert mountain country you can imagine. Here, they display tremendous loyalty to particular places, the herds living generation after generation on well-worn home grounds like the Scottish highland clans of old. These days one of the biggest problems facing bighorns are feral burros, which compete with the sheep for limited water and forage. Being large animals, bighorns periodically require significant amounts of water. So do burros. If it comes down to a question between burros and bighorns, it seems to me there is no question. I cannot leave the subject of desert bighorns here without recommending an indispensable book, *Counting Sheep: 20 Ways of Seeing Desert Bighorn*, edited by the respected desert ethnobotanist Gary Paul Nabhan. If you only have time for one essay, read the lead essay, 'Counting Sheep,' written by Doug Peacock. It will not disappoint.

The plants and animals that inhabit the deserts of North America are the ultimate survivors. They are tough and durable and they deserve our respect. When I was a professor, students used to ask me — why study the endangered species, animals such as the desert bighorn, the desert pupfish, the desert tortoise? In their lives and deaths, these animals, as nations and as individuals, have much to teach us about courage in the face of adversity, about freedom and responsibility, about the price we pay for over-specializing (as individuals, as corporations, again whatever metaphor you choose). Certain endangered species teach us, by example, that the generalist is often better equipped to survive times of change and upheaval than the specialist. Look at the persistent coyote that eats anything from mice to mule deer. And then consider the plight of the black-footed ferret that relies almost entirely on one food source, the prairie dog. When prairie dogs were exterminated by the stockmen, the black-footed ferret all but vanished. The coyote, on the other hand, kept running. And running.

Typical Chihuahuan Desert vegetation, southwestern Texas

So, I told them, specialize at your own risk. Heed the examples of nature. There are whole universities out there, with tenured professors that are desert toads, and deans that are black vultures. Lessons delivered hourly, by example, on all the virtues William Bennet extols. Libraries composed of the accumulated wisdom of a dozen dead civilizations, with living museums comprised of cliff dwellings and rock paintings, and outdoor amphitheaters built to hold one million, with nightly meteor showers and daily cloud shows that would put an IMAX show to shame. Squirming in their seats, the business majors would wonder if they could still drop the course.

Whatever the cost, we owe these fellow life forms an allegiance born of a common struggle and a shared future. Long may they all run, the whole bestiary, and long may they blossom, the entire herbal.

I I I

On January 16, 1832, Charles Darwin stopped for a few days on the Cape Verde Islands, about 400 miles west of Dakar, Senegal. The twenty-

Big-leafed sage, Great Basin Desert, northwestern Colorado

three-year-old geologist noticed that a peculiar dust fell continuously from the sky, coating everything on the *HMS Beagle* with a fine brown powder. This precipitation was sufficiently thick to obscure the horizons. According to the local residents, the dust occasionally became so dense that passing ships lost their way and grounded on outlying rocks and reefs. Mariners reported their sails had captured the strange grit as far as 1000 miles from the coast of Africa, and that the dust had been observed at points 1600 miles to the north and south of Africa. Darwin examined a sample under a microscope and observed sand, dirt and plant residue; a colleague later identified 67 microorganisms. The future author of *The Origin of Species*, as was his custom, formed a theory. His explanation was, like so many of his, extraordinarily simple: the dust had originated in the Sahara Desert and had been carried over the Atlas Mountains by the *harmattan*, or dry winter winds. Only in recent years have atmospheric physicists confirmed that the brown dust, as Darwin postulated, is in fact born in North Africa, carried across the Atlantic on strong westerlies, and then deposited like a fertilizer across the green jungles of the Amazon.

What does this historical anecdote tell us about deserts? Two things. First, we must remember — and this is especially relevant in the American Southwest — that much of the Sahara was not always, or even recently a desert. In fact, just 4,000 years ago much of the fauna we currently see in East and South Africa also occupied the savannas of North Africa. We know this from the fossil evidence and from cave artwork. Overgrazing by domesticated animals brought desertification to valley after valley. More recently, the Romans built 600 cities on the narrow coastal plain of *Africa Proconsularis*, exported half-a-million tons of wheat yearly, and replaced the resident wild grazers with hoofed locusts: goats and sheep. When the desert inevitably encroached as a result of deforestation and overgrazing, the Empire without "boundaries in space or time," as Virgil phrased it, lost its granary and collapsed into the eagerly awaiting hands of the barbarians.

Desertification, in short, can occur with lighting speed and is difficult, in some cases, impossible to reverse. The costs, in terms of lost agriculture and human life, can be immense. In this century African and Asian droughts have killed millions of people. The recent droughts that struck Ethiopia and Somalia had devastating costs, in terms of human suffering and social upheaval. Deserts, of course, can be formed both naturally and accidentally. In the first case, there is little we can do about it, but when formerly fertile lands are destroyed as a result of greed and stupidity, it is particularly tragic. Nature shows no mercy once the process of degradation begins. More often than not, the trend is irreversible, the effects permanent.

Chessler Park, Canyonlands National Park, Utah (Painted Desert)

Second, as Darwin's example illustrates, deserts can benefit the world in ways that are both obvious and not often immediately seen. The conversation on this subject usually begins with economics. The mineral resources of the world's deserts, so often buried under sand dunes and hidden along placer streams, are only partially known. What is known is that an immense wealth has already been extracted. Everyone knows about gypsum, common table salt, the borates. How many of us remember Ronald Reagan on television when we were kids, speaking on behalf of "20-mule team borax?" Not many realize that the total value of minerals extracted from the Searles Lake basin in California exceeds $1 billion. Elsewhere, bank accounts have swollen to eight and nine figures from gold and silver in Australia, oil in Libya, uranium in South Africa. Of course, mining is not very often benign — pay a visit to the open pit copper mine at Ajo, Arizona, just north of Organ Pipe National Monument, if you doubt the veracity of that statement.

Another reason for focusing discourse on desert areas is biodiversity, the web of plants and animals that collectively sustain life on earth. The rise of human civilization is deeply rooted in the earth. Deserts are a foundation ecosystem. Furthermore, the study of desert organisms often yields practical benefits to our species. The desert pupfish, for example, tolerates extremes of salinity and temperature that could have implications for treatment of human kidney disease. Nonaddictive painkillers can be developed from snake venom. Current research indicates that the buffalo gourd, a wild squash-like plant found in desert canyons, could be cultivated on the dry antelope prairie overlying the Ogallala acquifer. The plant requires little water, and all parts of it, including roots, gourds, vines, and seeds, can be put to use. If the Ogallala acquifer eventually dries up, the humble desert gourd may save local economies across Nebraska, Kansas, Wyoming and Colorado.

And so on.

There are so many other reasons to value deserts — aesthetic (Ansel Adams' career is one long tribute to the beauty of the Southwest), theological (the forty days spent by a carpenter in the desert wilderness completely transformed the history of western civilization), ethical (the land ethic of Aldo Leopold), commercial (20 million tourists in the deserts of California annually, each spending hundreds of dollars). In the end, you will each have to make your own choice.

As I say, the introduction to deserts was long ago. Much change since then. A couple of useless English degrees. A little shelf of nature books. Many dull and several enjoyable jobs. All but a handful of true friends come and gone. Two wives in and out of the house. Several other lovers screeching down the driveway, most happily forgotten. Mountains climbed, valleys crossed. A son growing like a sapling in the shade. Much change. And yet I still have this passion for the desert, keep going back, year after year. I think that it will last all the days of my life, this *affaire de couer*, and that is fine with me. Everyone should have such a place, whose freedom they would defend as their own, because they are the same thing. Something will have gone out of us as a people, something more than a few sunburned acres of cactus and creosote, if we ever stop loving these desert places. In the end it comes to this: a slender book created to recruit you, dear reader, into the dusty ranks of those defending the deserts. Now, fellow desert rats, onward into our beloved ratlands.

I

The Mojave Desert

East away from the Sierras, south from Panamint
and Amargosa, east and south many an uncount-
ed mile, is the Country of Lost Borders...Desert
is a loose term to indicate land that supports no
man; whether the land can be bitted and broken
to that purpose not yet proven. Void of life it
never is, however dry the air and villainous the
soil...for all the toll the desert takes of a man it
gives compensations, deep breaths, deep sleep,
and the communion of the stars. It comes upon
one with new force in the pauses of the night
that Chaldeans were a desert-bred people.
                                        —Mary Austin,
                        The Land of Little Rain (1903)

THE POPULAR IMAGE OF SOUTHERN CALIFORNIA is of gridlocked freeways, oppressive smog, and urban sprawl. A realm where hedonism has been
elevated to the stature of a philosophical school, and vanity mirrors are the
chief artifact of a minor religion. Where pit bulls rule the side streets and
gun-toting teenagers prove William Golding was right when he wrote *Lord
of the Flies.* Where various unpredictable natural disasters provide the general
nihilistic atmosphere of an American Pompeii waiting to happen. For many
thousands of square miles along the coast, this is the congested, dyspeptic,
and ominous state of affairs. Drive a few hours to the east, though, and you
will be transported to another world: skies clear as glass, a great cleansing
wash of high altitude sunlight, sharply faulted mountains, rolling sun-

Hedgehog cactus, Mojave Desert (California)

bleached dune fields, the beds of ancient lakes, immense lava flows, weathered escarpments, smoothly sculpted boulders of plutonic gneiss. Here is a sanctuary for the human spirit, as well as a refuge for fauna and flora found nowhere else on earth.

Despite hosting over 20 million visitors annually, the Mojave Desert offers as much beauty and solitude as I have found in the most remote regions of Alaska and northern Canada. How? For one thing the desert is enormous — in excess of 25 million acres. Consider that for a moment. Twenty-five million acres is an area larger than the states of New Hampshire, Vermont, Massachusetts, Connecticut, and New Jersey combined! For another, most Californians and vacationers prefer the diversions of Santa Monica Boulevard and Venice Beach. That leaves the high desert for nature aficionados. In the Mojave, you can drive for 100 miles (as on the deserted backroads from Twenty-Nine Palms to Amboy and Kelso) and see just a handful of other cars. Set out on foot, and you walk back in time ten thousand years, to an age when the desert was inhabited only by sheep with horns bleached the color of sand and shy, darting lizards forever chasing ants.

Geographically, the Mojave Desert is part of the basin and range country, which ranges from northern Mexico to southern Oregon. This expansive region is characterized by over 150 broad valleys and 160 north-to-south-trending mountain ranges. Precipitation rarely exceeds nine to ten inches. Winters can be chilly, with snow at the higher elevations, but summers are

just plain hot. At Death Valley, temperatures as high as 134 degrees
Fahrenheit have been recorded. Surface water is scarce to nonexistent.
Despite the harsh surroundings life endures, even flourishes here, from wild
palm oases to pinyon-juniper woodlands, from cholla cactus gardens to
Joshua tree parklands, from squeaking pocket mice to singing poorwills.

As is often the case, we have only a fragmentary picture of the first
Mojaveans. In a few places, such as the scattered palm springs of Joshua Tree
National Park, evidence of their subsistence lifestyles remain: mortar holes
ground into boulders and ledges, broken pottery in canyons and caverns,
arrowheads and spear points near game ambush sites. The climate was
cooler and wetter in the distant past, and the desert was a more friendly
place to live than it is now. In the latter decades of the sixteenth century the
cross-bearing Spaniards arrived in California, and it was not long before
they ventured out on the Mojave in pursuit of gold, trading routes and souls
to convert. Quite often their encounters with the natives were not entirely
benign for the natives, or for
the Spanish. In 1776, for
example, Father Francesco
Garces, a contemporary of
the more famous Dominguez
and Escalante, praised his
loyal Mojave guides for lead-
ing him safely through the
desert, but five years later
was unexpectedly sent to
heaven by the less hospitable
Yuma Indians. In sum,
although the Spanish utilized
various trails and "roads" in
the Mojave, their settlements
in Southern California were
primarily confined to the
coast, especially around San
Diego and in the Los
Angeles basin.

The first American to
encounter the Mojave was
the irrepressible Jedediah
Smith, who followed the
Virgin River past its conflu-

Quartz monzonite rock formation,
Joshua Tree National Park (California)

Close-up of Joshua tree blossom, Mojave Desert (California)

ence with the Colorado to the Mojave Indian villages near present-day Needles, California. Smith then journeyed west across the high desert to the coast. This was on his legendary reconnaissance of 1826–1829. Later, the frontiersman Joseph Walker explored a more northerly portion of the Mojave Desert in 1833. It was not until the expedition of John Fremont (1843–1844) that the Mojave Desert was observed by an experienced naturalist and scientist. Fremont was struck by the beauty and potential of California, and wrote about it in the manner of a real estate agent. He trekked over the Mojave Desert from west to east, and passed through what would one day be the suburbs of Las Vegas (what a difference a century makes). Just five years later, with the discovery of gold in the new state of California, thousands of Forty-Niners crossed the Mojave Desert in search of fortune. During this same decade, Secretary of War Jefferson Davis (the same who later formed the Confederacy) dispatched a Pacific Railroad survey into the Mojave, seeking a southerly route for the first transcontinental railroad. The George Wheeler Survey of 1869–1879 further explored the high desert, including a penetration of extraterrestrial Death Valley.

    With the appearance of the Southern Pacific Railroad to the south the Mojave came to be occupied by something more than grizzled prospectors, perennial outcasts and minor outlaws. Large-scale mining (gold, silver, iron, borax) brought boomtowns and larger populations to the region. Subsequently, the construction of Route 66 across the Mojave attracted even more settlers. This was especially the case during the Dust Bowl years of the 1930s when the desperate "Okies" immortalized in John Steinbeck's *The Grapes of Wrath* used the road to reach the "Arcady" of southern and central California. World War II brought the establishment of various army, marine and air force bases in the Mojave. In the 1940s, General Patton trained his armored units in the area. To this day, the tracks of tank treads can be seen in the desert.

Gradually, in a scene that has been repeated from Plymouth Rock (Pilgrim landfall, 1620) to the sandy red deserts of Mars (Viking spacecraft landing, 1976), American civilization was putting its fingerprints all over the landscape. One of the most important events in this respect occurred just after World War II, when Las Vegas, Nevada was developed as an entertainment and legalized gambling mecca. Reno, up north in the Great Basin Desert, later followed suit. Marilyn Monroe's last film, *The Misfits* (1961), dramatized the human alienation and suffering brought on by the Nevada casino lifestyle, with a script written by her Pulitzer-prize winning husband Arthur Miller. Clark Gable gave perhaps the best performance of his career as the broken-down cowboy forced by circumstances to round up the last wild horses for the slaughterhouse. It was ironically his final film as well.

Of the Mojave military bases, none have been of greater importance than the Nevada Test Site. Much of the nuclear testing conducted by the Department of Defense during the Cold War occurred at this location. The area is classic basin and range topography, with three primary features — Frenchman Valley, Jackass Flats, and Yucca Valley. As in other parts of the Mojave, creosote fills the valleys, with sagebrush and cactus in the foothills, and pinyon pine and juniper at higher elevations. Over the years, hundreds of nuclear tests took place at the site, both above ground (until President Kennedy banned them in 1963) and below ground (until President Clinton suspended them in 1995). Though the public is not generally aware of it, underground nuclear explosions also occurred near Carlsbad in southeastern New Mexico, near Farmington, New Mexico, in the vicinity of Grand Valley and Rifle in western Colorado, on Amchitka Island in the Aleutians, and, of all places, in a salt dome near Hattiesburg, Mississippi. Some believe we poisoned our environment, and in some cases our citizenry, with deadly radioactivity for little gain. Others make the contrary argument that we were in a

GETTING THERE

Nevada Test Site: The enormous reservation is located about 80 miles northwest of Las Vegas and about 75 miles east of Death Valley National Park.

Joshua tree in blossom, early spring, Mojave Desert (California)

state of war, and that the repeated testing of these weapons was essential to national security.

Nye County, Nevada, in which the Nevada Test Site is located, has been the center of a political firestorm in the 1990s. On October 23, 1995, Nye County was the subject of a *Time* magazine cover story entitled "Don't Tread on Me: An Inside Look at the West's Growing Rebellion." The leaders of the grass-roots uprising believe the federal government owns too much land in the west. In Nye County, for example, which is over 18,000 square miles in size (larger than Vermont and New Hampshire), the military, Forest Service and BLM "own" 93 percent of the land. Those who live on the other 7 percent want more for themselves, and challenge the treaties and agreements by which the government (i.e. the American people) own the land. In 1995, the Justice Department reported that at least 35 counties in Nevada, Arizona, California and New Mexico had passed so-called "take-back" laws that declare federal ownership of the lands to be null and void. In some cases there have been acts of violence, such as bombings, against federal offices and officials. This movement is one to be closely watched, with the potential to seriously impact the deserts. As the national debt increases, it is likely that pressure will grow to sell the public lands. If this were to occur, it would be the final disgrace in a Greek tragedy of national excess and political ineptitude.

Like the much larger Great Basin Desert to the north, the Mojave Desert is dominated by shrubs. At the lower elevations the hardy, indestructible creosote prevails. Also prevalent are various cactuses (barrel, prickly pear, cholla), sagebrush, and brittlebrush. Each spring the brittlebush brightens up the desert with cheerful yellow flowers. (Wordsworth had his English daffodils, desert lovers have the brittlebush). In the old days, brittlebush provided an aromatic resin that was burned as incense by priests. The Indians — and this says so much about the differences between the two cultures — used the resin as chewing gum. Mojave yucca is another distinctive plant of this desert. In years of good rainfall, the yucca produces impossibly thick clusters of ivory white flowers, immaculate bouquets fit for any wedding party. No doubt the Joshua tree is the plant most often associated with the Mojave (more on them in the Joshua Tree National Park section). They are one of the most widespread species in the Mojave. I have found them hiding like hermits in the timbered foothills of the San Bernadino Mountains, miles from anything resembling a desert, and I have walked among their crowded ranks in the sun-baked hills of Mojave National Preserve, miles from anything resembling a mountain range. They are the very essence of this hard, lonely, cruel, gentle, resourceful and surprisingly rich desert.

View from Land's End, Joshua Tree National Park (California)

Animals abound here but, as in any desert, only at night. Drive around after dark and you might see a desert bighorn sheep (in your dreams) or a mountain lion (also unlikely). More in the realm of reality are harvester ants (don't laugh — these are, according to Professor Edward O. Wilson, among the most important animals in the world), rattlesnakes (take your pick — Mojave, Great Basin, Sidewinder, Speckled), ground squirrels (carry the plague and hanta virus — keep moving), mule deer, and, of course, the ubiquitous coyote and his best friend the black-tailed jackrabbit (why Jack, and not Tom or Billy?). These are animals who have much to teach us about surviving in an arid environment, if any of us want to take the time to sit and watch them.

The Mojave is my favorite desert. Opportunities for my two favorite pastimes, hiking and photography, are unsurpassed. The desert also lends itself for another cherished pursuit — long periods of idle contemplation. Public lands abound. Winters are mild, even hot at times. Springs and autumns are sublime. Major airports in Los Angeles, Las Vegas, and San Diego make a short, restorative visit as easy as finding a bargain ticket and hopping on a plane (I always fly into L.A. at night, in order to more easily navigate the nerve-wracking freeways). Once in the desert, you can be

Queen's Valley, Joshua Tree National Park (California)

alone for days, or find a public campground and enjoy the good company. For those who love a brilliant desert sunset, the beauty of a cactus blossom, the song of a canyon wren, the howl of a coyote, the surprising green of a desert oasis, there is no finer place. In the wild deserts of Turkestan you'd have to contend with sand cobras. Curious lion prides stalk the sun-baked deserts of Namibia. Else-where, deserts host volatile border wars or provide sanctuary for rov-ing bands of land pirates. Here, in America's smallest major desert, there is only peace and quiet, beauty and solitude, all possible because of the public lands, because of American generosity, optimism, and reverence for life.

Cholla and desert sky, Mojave National Preserve (California)

STILL LIFE WITH ROCKS: JOSHUA TREE NATIONAL PARK

I support a positive philosophy of life and art. Wherever this leads me, I am sure it is further than were I a practising pessimist! I frankly profess a somewhat mystical concept of nature; I believe the world is incomprehensibly beautiful — an endless prospect of magic and wonder.

—Ansel Adams, from his Commencement
Address, Occidental College, 1961

In 1844 Western explorer John C. Fremont, traveling in the Mojave Desert, called the Joshua tree "the most repulsive tree in the vegetable king-dom." A few years later the Mormons passed through. They thought the uplifted branches evoked the arms of Joshua beckoning them toward the promised land. Thus the name was born. The Joshua tree, a member of the

Teddy bear cholla at sunrise, Mojave Desert (California)

lily family, is actually an oversized yucca. The "trees" cover the highlands of 630,800-acre Joshua Tree National Park, which was designated a national park in 1994 (the area had been established as a national monument in 1937).

Visitors find the park's symbol and namesake to be either grotesque or exquisite, depending on the point of view. The first impression is of top-heaviness. Imagine the muscular arms of a heavyweight boxer like Joe Frazier set on the compact body of a marathon runner like Frank Shorter. At the end of each stout branch are heavy daggerlike leaves. In early spring, after a wet winter, the branch tips visibly droop with heavy, ivory blossom clusters. These lovely flowers have a subtle sweet odor that attracts butterflies, moths, birds, various rodents and reptiles, deer, all manner of ants, and legions of nature photographers and artists.

Although Joshua Tree is named for a plant, it is also a refuge for birds, with such species as the roadrunner and raven, phainopepla and loggerhead shrike, Gambel's quail and golden eagle. The Scott's oriole, a beautiful yellow and black feathered bird, is common in the Joshua tree woodlands. At oases such as Cottonwood Spring and Lost Palms you will hear the song of the canyon wren in the day and, if you stay late enough, the hoot of the burrowing or barn owl. At night during the breeding season, you might also hear the melancholy lament of the poor-will, which sounds just like its name.

Turkey vultures are often seen, circling on thermals as they search for road kills and other easy meals.

Evidence of past human activities are scattered here and there over the park. Indians, who gathered mesquite beans, cactus fruit and pinyon nuts as they were seasonably available in the highlands, left little evidence of their passage over the area (which is nice considering what has followed in the Mojave). Spanish explorers also left few reminders of their tenure in the region. Beginning in the 1870s, various cattlemen had begun to run Texas longhorn cattle in what is today the park. Looking at the "range" today, especially if you are from a place like Georgia, you can only shake your head. There is a type of bunchgrass here, but it is not much compared to the pastures of the east, even the east of west Texas. The cattlemen, who included a few rustlers, left various water catchments such as Barker Dam, as testament of their attempts to "tame" the desert. Later came the miners, and you can find their old claims at such places as the Lost Horse Mine, which is accessed on the road to Keys View. Believe it or not, there were also homesteaders who came here to settle.

There are actually two desert ecosystems in Joshua Tree. Above 3000 feet, more in the northern range of the park, you will find the Mojave desert, with the ubiquitous Joshua tree. This is a cooler, wetter habitat. Below 3000 feet is the Colorado Desert, a much drier desert associated with creosote bush, stands of ocotillo and cholla cactus. The two deserts are both similar and different in appearance, like a brother and a sister from the same family. Although they cope with much of the same factors — heat, water stress, cool to cold winters — their environments are slightly different and thus have produced slightly different adaptations and communities. Pinto Basin, just south of Queen Valley, is the area where the transition

Cottonwood Spring, Joshua Tree National Park (California)

GETTING THERE

Access to **Joshua Tree National Park** is either from Interstate 10 at the Cottonwood Spring exit 51 miles east of Palm Springs, or from State Route 62, 20 miles north of Palm Springs. The Visitor's Center is located one mile east of Twentynine Palms on the park road south to Cottonwood Spring. This is 16 miles east of the first park entrance on State Route 62.

occurs. As you approach the famous cholla cactus garden, you are leaving the Mojave behind and entering the Colorado (which, of course, is a province of the Sonoran).

I must confess that Joshua Tree is one of my favorite desert parks, primarily because of the numerous photographic possibilities. The rock formations (especially the quartz monzonite boulders crosscut with dikes of aplite) and the unusual plants (those strangely contorted Joshua trees) always make a visit to the park something special. I'm always sorry to leave, and anxious to return. It is a crowded place in the spring but, as in any park, fifteen minutes from the road, you'll be all by yourself. There are places where even rock climbers don't go (the park is legendary among rock climbers), and once in those secret retreats you can sit for an hour, or a morning, or all day, and let the desert slowly come to you. It comes as a curious leopard lizard, or as a coyote out on patrol, or as a honeybee investigating your red bandanna for evidence of pollen. If you wait a very long time, you may see one of the rarer inhabitants — a desert tortoise or a desert bighorn. If so, consider yourself lucky. These are two of the old grandfathers for whom this place is not a hostile wilderness but a well-traveled home. They have much to teach about persistence, resilience, flexibility, and simple endurance.

 ## POINTS OF INTEREST

BARKER DAM — Barker Dam, constructed earlier in the century, is located off the Loop Road just east of the Hidden Valley Campground. A small pond forms behind this historic dam, and at dusk and dawn the environs of the pond are a good place for wildlife viewing.

COTTONWOOD SPRING — Located in the vicinity of the Cottonwood Visitor Center, Cottonwood Spring has been visited by people for many thousands of years. Boulders in the area were used by Indians for grinding seeds and fruits and some still reveal distinct hollows from years of use. From 1870 through 1910, the spring was a welcome resting spot for miners, freight haulers, and overland travelers. There are several large cottonwood trees at the spring, as well as native California fan palms. The trail to Lost Palms oasis begins at Cottonwood Spring. Parking spots at the end of the road tend to fill up quickly, so plan to begin your hike early (before 9 or 10 a.m.) during the peak spring and fall seasons. Cottonwood Spring is a popular place for birdwatching and also, along the south-facing slopes, for observing early (March) spring wildflowers.

Leaves of California fan palms, Mojave Desert (California)

CHOLLA CACTUS GARDEN —The cholla cactus garden, one of the most interesting sites in Joshua Tree, is located on the main park road about halfway between the Oasis Visitor Center and the Cottonwood Visitor Center. A short nature trail guides visitors through the many bigelow cactuses found in this unique area. Stay on the path and be careful not to touch the many-spined cholla pads. If they become attached to your shoes or trousers, use pens or pencils to pry them loose. Do not attempt to touch them. You can also see creosote bush, jojoba (pronounced *ho-HO-bah*), sacred datura, beavertail cactus, and pencil cholla here. In the spring listen for the song of the cactus wren, which build their nests among the protective spines of the cholla cactus.

FORTYNINE PALMS OASIS — The trail to Fortynine Palms Oasis is located at the end of Canyon Road about five miles west of Twentynine Palms on State Route 62. A stand of native California fan palms, somewhat charred from a recent wildfire, are found here.

GEOLOGY TOUR ROAD — The Geology Tour Road, perhaps the most impressive of its kind in the national park system, leads visitors from the loop road in Queen Valley south across the Little San Bernadino Mountains to the vicinity of Indio, east of Palm Desert. Four-wheel-drive vehicles are recommended for this 18-mile self-guided excursion through rugged backcountry. Along the way you will see dramatic formations of quartz monzonite and pinto gneiss (pronounced *nice*), basaltic peaks, dry washes and alluvial fans, faulted valleys, dry lakes or playas, abandoned gold mines, and ancient petroglyphs.

HIDDEN VALLEY — Approximately twelve miles east of the West Entrance Station is Hidden Valley, a spectacular region of massive quartz monzonite boulders and open-canopied Joshua tree woodlands, with many good hiking trails. In earlier times, cattle rustlers used this area to hide their stolen livestock.

JUMBO ROCKS PICNIC GROUND — One of my favorite places for photography is Jumbo Rocks, which is found on the loop road just east of Queen Valley. The large and unusually shaped boulders of quartz monzonite, together with the classic Mojave vegetation and distant vistas, make for striking compositions. Be careful not to climb the rocks, as a fall could prove a little more than unfortunate.

KEYS VIEW — Accessed by the park loop road south of Lost Horse Valley, Keys View offers a commanding vista of the western Mojave Desert, including the beautiful Coachella Valley and the distant snow-capped peaks of the San Jacinto Mountains.

LOST HORSE MINE — Located east of the road to Keys View, the 2-mile trail to Lost Horse Mine provides visitors with a look at a vintage gold mine, a prospecting site that evokes scenes in *The Treasure of the Sierra Madre.*

LOST PALMS OASIS — The Lost Palms Oasis is one of the most popular day hikes in the park, if not in the Mojave. Expect crowds here. The 4-mile trail (8 miles round-trip) leads hikers over rocky ridges and small canyons to a lovely assemblage of over 100 native California fan palms. An intermittent stream (not suitable for drinking) runs through the grove.

Lost Palms Oasis, Joshua Tree National Park (California)

Wildlife, including desert bighorn sheep, are sometimes seen in and around the oasis.

OASIS OF MARA — The visitor center for the north end of the park is located near the Oasis of Mara, which was used in prehistoric times by Indians and during more recent historic times by prospectors.

RYAN MOUNTAIN — One of the best hiking trails in the park leads 1.5 miles up Ryan Mountain, where great views are afforded of Queen Valley and Lost Horse Valley. The trail begins on the loop road just west of the Sheep Pass campground.

LONESOME TRIANGLE:
MOJAVE NATIONAL PRESERVE

…the terrible desert, where the distance shimmers and the black cinder mountains hang unbearably in the distance.
> —John Steinbeck, *The Grapes of Wrath*

The Mojave National Preserve is located north of Joshua Tree National Park and south of Death Valley National Park. Local residents refer to the area as the "The Lonesome Triangle" because, like a crude Euclidean figure, the preserve is roughly bounded on the east by the Nevada state line and on the west by Interstates 15 and 40. In this expansive country of over one million acres are enormous dune fields, extinct volcanoes, deeply eroded canyons, fossil lake beds, intermittent streams and rivers, and ancient rugged mountains. No matter where you stand in the East Mojave, you will always be in the presence of dramatic mountain ranges. They are everywhere, each aligned in the north to south direction so characteristic of the basin and range country. These mountains are especially spectacular at dawn and dusk, silhouetted sharply against the wine-colored desert sky. It is a silent, austere country, fit for

GETTING THERE

The **Mojave National Preserve** is an immense wilderness set between Interstate 40, Interstate 20 and the Nevada border. It can be entered at a number of points, including the Essex exit on Interstate 40, which provides access to the Providence Mountains State Recreational Area, and old Route 66, which runs from Essex west through Amboy to Ludlow (roughly parallel to Interstate 40).

Yellow brittlebush in spring, Providence Mountains State Park (California)

deep thought and contemplation. At night, far beyond the city lights, the stars evoke the ancient poetry of another desert: "Canst thou bind the sweet influences of Pleiades, or loose the bands of Orion? Canst thou bring forth Mazzaroth in his season? Or canst thou guide Arcturus with his sons? Knowest thou the ordinances of heaven? Canst thou set the dominion thereof in the earth?" (Job)

> (NOTE: For road travel in the Mojave, I would recommend that you purchase *Southern & Central California Atlas & Gazetteer,* which is one of a national series published by DeLorme Press, PO 298-5500, Freeport, Maine 04032. The book presents a very helpful collection of detailed topographic maps, costs only $14.95 and can be ordered at 1-800-227-1656, ext. 5500.)

 ## POINTS OF INTEREST

AFTON CANYON — Though not formally part of the Mojave National Preserve, Afton Canyon is an interesting and easily accessible site. About 30 miles east of Barstow on Interstate 15 take the Afton exit and follow the three mile access road to the BLM campground at the mouth of the canyon. The gorge formed by the Mojave River, which runs in all but the most serious droughts, is spectacular; some have gone so far as to call it the Grand Canyon of the Mojave.

CIMA DOME —The major attraction of Cima Dome, a 75-square-mile region of volcanic uplifting, is the extensive Joshua tree forest. Access is from the Cima Road exit on Interstate 15 about 30 miles east of the Nevada state line. The Cima Road provides an excellent auto tour of the basin and range topography so much associated with the Mojave.

KELSO DUNES — The Kelso Dunes are one of the most beautiful features of the Mojave Desert. Located north of the Old Dad Mountains and south of the Devil's Playground, the dune field covers approximately 45 square miles and attains heights of 700 feet. Access is via a gravel road east of Kelbaker Road to the old Kelso Depot. To reach Kelbaker Road take the Kelso Depot/Granite Pass exit on Interstate 40 and head north.

ROUTE 66 — Certainly one of the most historic roads in the twentieth century, Route 66 cuts from east to west across the heart of Mojave Desert. The refugees of the Dust Bowl in the 1930s knew Route 66 well. They had little choice when the Great Plains were turned into a desert as a result of poor agricultural practices and persistent drought. One of the most easily accessible portions of Route 66 runs through Bagdad and Amboy south of Interstate 40 and north of the Twentynine Palms Marine Corps Base. The Amboy crater can be viewed from a marked side road running south from Route 66 just west of Amboy.

PROVIDENCE MOUNTAINS STATE RECREATION AREA — The Providence Mountains, accessed by a state road that runs 23 miles north from Interstate 40, near Essex, California, represent some of the highest mountains in the east

Spring flowers at Death Valley National Park (California)

Mojave, with altitudes ranging from 3,400 to 7,171 feet. The heights
provide excellent views of the desert. On a clear day you can see south to
the Hualapai Mountains in Arizona, nearly 100 miles distant. Two sites
bear mentioning: the Mitchell Caverns and the Mary Beal Nature Study
Trail. Both are located at the state recreation area north of the Essex exit
on Interstate 40. The caverns include limestone formations, with stalagmites, stalactites, and helictites. Park rangers are available to provide
guided tours, which last about 90 minutes (the caves are closed from
mid-June through mid-September). Six campsites are available. Near the
Mitchell Caverns Visitor's Center is the Mary Beal Nature Study Trail,
which offers a close-up view of such common Mojave plants as creosote,
cholla, prickly pear cactus, Mojave yucca, pinyon pine, pancake cactus,
hedgehog cactus, barrel cactus, blue sage, and desert fir. Desert bighorn
sheep are sometimes seen in this area.

IMAGES OF ETERNITY:
DEATH VALLEY NATIONAL PARK

I was camped in my car near Stovepipe Wells, usually sleeping on
top of my car on the camera platform, which measured about 5 x
9 feet. Arising long before dawn, I made some coffee and reheated
some beans, then gathered my equipment and started on the
rather arduous walk through the dunes to capture the legendary
dune sunrise.

—Ansel Adams,
Examples: The Making of 40 Photographs

A trip to Death Valley National Park is like a journey to another world.
Why? Because much of the park possess so little chlorophyll, so few signs of
plant or animal life. After awhile your eyes begin to ache for some green, a
sign of photosynthesis, of life. Picture the following scene: sun-baked rock
plains, blindingly bright salt basins, hulking mountains half-buried in their
own rubble, gigantic alluvial fans covered with primordial gravel, an empty
stretch of shimmering blacktop, a darkly polarized sky (sunglasses and a hat
are *de rigeur*) without a cloud or even the hint of a cloud. That is Death
Valley. And in that austerity, I suppose, is its strong attraction and special
beauty. Death Valley presents the aspect of an alien, inhospitable world —
the deserts of Mars or the sunbaked side of one of the far Jovian moons.
Hundreds of years from now our descendants will travel to Mars and other

Salt flats, Death Valley National Park (California)

worlds. In Death Valley you can catch a glimpse of what they will encounter. The desolate landscape also presents a vision of the future, ages hence, after the sun has gone supernovae and deep-fried the first three planets.

The Mojave's most famous national park comprises over three million acres, which makes it the largest national park outside of Alaska. Elevations in the park range from 282 feet below sea level at Badwater to 11,049 feet on Telescope Peak. At the higher elevations fir, spruce and quaking aspen are found, but at lower elevations, which is most of the park, plants are either in short supply or conspicuously abscent. You will see a lot of creosote, and in spring, flowers such as milkweed and desert sunflower. Vast regions of the park consist of salt pans that stretch for miles, sand dune fields, deeply eroded canyons, colorful cliffs, and rugged and seldom visited mountain ranges.

The geological history of Death Valley is immense. The marble in Mosaic Canyon dates back to nearly 1.5 billion years ago. That is a long time before Moses and Ramses, not to mention Voltaire and Rousseau. Elsewhere the rocks are more recent, with volcanic flows that are mere teenagers of only 30 or 35 million years in age. All of this

Joshua trees at sunset, near Old Dad Mountains, Mojave National Preserve (California)

Quartz monzonite boulder, dry streambed, Mojave Desert (California)

geology is what attracted the first miners to the area. At sites like Skidoo in the Panamints, hardy desperate forgotten souls spent the best years of their lives digging for gold. The real wealth of Death Valley, though, was borax, which was deeply accumulated in the ancient lake beds. In the 1870s William Coleman of San Francisco began his famous 20-mule teams, which carried the borax to Mojave. At Furnace Creek Ranch you can see some of the well-worn equipment from this now near-mythological age at the Borax Museum.

Geologists define Death Valley as a *graben*, or a sunken portion of land between two faulted mountains. At its greatest length, Death Valley is 190 miles long, with widths that vary from five to twenty miles. Toward the east are the Grapevine and Funeral ranges, and to the west the equally stark Panamints. The dramatic manner in which these three

Scorpion, Mojave Desert
Photo courtesy of National Park Service

mountain ranges rise from the floor of the valley, with little in the way of preliminary foothills, adds to the austere beauty of the area. Because Death Valley is around 280 feet below sea level, with no major vegetation to relieve the effects of solar radiation, the area becomes incredibly hot, with recorded ground temperatures of nearly 200 degrees Fahrenheit. The relative abundance of life in such desolate conditions is a powerful testament to the ingenuity and resilience of nature.

One of the chief problems at Death Valley National Park are feral burros. They are descended from burros formerly used by prospectors and miners to transport equipment and ore. Currently these indefatigable beasts of burden are roaming widely in the roadless areas of the park, competing with native desert bighorn for scarce resources of food and water. This is particularly the case around isolated springs. For some people the solution to these non-native pests seems simple, inexpensive, and obvious — bullets from a helicopter. For others, sympathy with any life forms, even livestock unnatural and destructive to the habitat, precludes such action. The park service currently conducts periodic round-ups, in an attempt to reduce numbers, but this has not proven a permanent solution to the problem.

Without a doubt, the best time to visit Death Valley is in the spring (March/April), both because of the mild temperatures and wildflower displays. Even on the lowest flats you will see beautiful flowers such as sand verbena and primose. This was one of Ansel Adams' favorite locations, and for good reason. Death Valley offers some of the most unusual scenes in the Mojave, with striking textural patterns resulting from the complex and deeply eroded geological formations, and rare opportunities for compositions based on stark line and form. The sand dunes at Stovepipe Wells are always a favorite, as is the bizarre terrain around Devil's Golf Course. Both are best at sunrise and sunset. A photographer could spend weeks here, and never exhaust the possibilities. Generally, I have found the longer I spend in a place, the better the photographs are when I get back

GETTING THERE

Death Valley National Park: Main access is either from Las Vegas or Los Angeles. From Las Vegas, take U.S. 95 north to Beatty (about 120 miles), Nevada, and turn left on State 374, which leads across the Amargosa Desert and the Funeral Mountains into the heart of the park. Approaching from Los Angeles, the best route would be north on Interstate 15 through Barstow to Baker (about 100 miles from Los Angeles). At Baker, turn north on State 127. Just past Shoshone (about 56 miles north), a turn to the west on State 178 takes you into the southern range of Death Valley.

Mojave yucca blossom in early spring, Mojave Desert (California)

home. Time is required to find the best shooting locations, and then patience for the light and shadowing to be just right. And then a bit of luck.

In the end, Death Valley is *sui generis*. A realm unlike any other, except perhaps the Dead Sea region of Israel (which is even further below sea level). Death Valley is a place where life has been largely stripped away, and the original surface of the earth can be seen, naked and bare, in its pure and elementary shapes, as in the pages of Euclid's geometry. Line, form and color reign here. Not man, or woman, or nation. There are rocks in Death Valley that were formed when life first trafficked in the tides of the moon, and mountain ranges that will still be standing when our species has met its ultimate fate. Let insincerity and ambition reign elsewhere. Death Valley will forever be the domain of the sun and the sand, the wind and the rock, a landscape from the proverbs of Heraclitus or the pages of Thomas Merton.

 ## POINTS OF INTEREST

ARTIST'S DRIVE — A beautiful loop drive of around 10 miles located south of Furnace Creek on Highway 178. Many photographic possibilities here, as the name suggests.

DANTE'S VIEW — This fantastic overlook is located south of Highway 190 and is accessed by the well-marked road just west of Travertine Point. A good hour-and-a-half round trip from the main road, including a short walk.

DARWIN FALLS — Located in the vicinity of Father Crowley Point (see below). Follow Highway 190 for another seven miles to the access road, which leads to the trailhead. This is one of the few true oases in the park, replete with willow and cottonwood trees.

EUREKA DUNES — Located almost 14 miles west of the Panamint Spring Resort on Highway 190. You turn north on the Saline Valley Road and then follow the signs for about 9 miles to the stand of Joshua trees.

FATHER CROWLEY POINT — Located on Highway 190 near Rainbow Canyon, Father Crowley Point offers visitors traveling east their first panoramic view of the park. The point includes a fine prospect of Panamint Valley and the Panamint Range.

GOLDEN CANYON TRAIL — A five-mile loop trail leads through this scenic area near Zabriskie Point a few miles south of Furnace Creek on Highway 190 (maps available at the Visitor Center).

FURNACE CREEK — Furnace Creek looks like a sheik's winter palace from the Saudi Arabian peninsula — tall palm trees, flower gardens, swimming pools, an 18-hole golf course, six tennis courts, fine restaurants, luxury hotel — all set in the middle of North America's lowest desert. At Furnace Creek there is a national park office and visitor's center (619-786-2331), as well as a campground. For more information on the resort contact: Furnace Creek Inn & Ranch, PO Box 1, Death Valley, California 92328 (619-786-2307).

Spring wildflowers and yucca blossom, Mojave Desert (California)

Beavertail cactus blossoms, Mojave Desert (California)

HARMONY BORAX WORKS — Located just two miles north of the Visitor Center on Highway 190, this historic site includes adobe ruins, equipment and a wagon from the 1880 mining period.

MOSAIC CANYON — This canyon offers one of the better day hiking experiences in Death Valley National Park. In places at the upper end you'll have to crawl over small, dry waterfalls (obviously not a trail to hike if thunderstorms threaten). The exposed marble along the canyon walls is over one billion years old and in places is worn to a beautiful smooth surface. Round trip is about 8 miles. Road access is 3 miles off Highway 190, just west of Stovepipe Wells. The access road can be difficult.

OTHER SITES

ANTELOPE VALLEY CALIFORNIA POPPY RESERVE — Some of the most spectacular wildflower displays in Southern California are found at this location. Each spring, in March and April, outdoor photographers from around the country converge at Antelope Valley. If you want to meet them all at one place and one time, Antelope Valley is the spot (as is Denali's Wonder Lake for the summer solstice, or Yellowstone's Tower Junction for the September elk bugling season). Located west of Lancaster, California on the north side of Lancaster Road (PO Box 1171, Lancaster, California 93584).

ANTELOPE VALLEY INDIAN MUSEUM — An interesting little museum in the old Edwards house (Edwards was a collector of Indian artifacts) located east of Lancaster, California near the corner of Avenue M and 165th Street East (PO Box 1171, Lancaster, California 93584).

DESERT NATIONAL WILDLIFE REFUGE — The refuge is located just north of Las Vegas with access via U.S. 95. It protects the largest population (nearly 1,000) of desert bighorn sheep, which flourish within the wild peaks and canyons of the expansive refuge. Here, too, are such rare and endangered animals as the desert tortoise, gila monster, and kit fox. Bob Marshall, writing in the 1930s, called this area the finest desert wilderness in the country. He would probably be delighted that the refuge protects this unique ecosystem, but dismayed about years of radiation exposure from the nuclear test site just to the west (702-384-3466).

DESERT WOODLAND STATE PARK — Located just up the road from Antelope Valley California Poppy Reserve near Palmdale, California. The park was established to protected an unusual assemblage of Joshua trees and junipers. To reach Desert Woodland, continue on another 5 miles on the Lancaster Road from the Poppy Reserve (PO Box 1408, Lancaster, California 93584).

MOORTEN BOTANICAL GARDEN — Located at 1701 South Palm Canyon Drive in Palm Springs, California, the garden contains thousands of desert plant species from sites around the world. The arboretum is also a bird preserve (619-327-6555).

PALM SPRINGS DESERT MUSEUM — Exhibits feature both the natural and human history of the Mojave Desert. The museum is located at 101 Museum Drive in Palm Springs, California (619-325-0189).

RED ROCK CANYON STATE PARK — The opening sequence of *Jurassic Park* was filmed at this location, which is often used as a backdrop for westerns and science fiction movies. Colorful sedimentary and igneous formations make Red Rock Canyon a special place, especially in the spring when wild-flowers add to the beauty. Good hiking trails abound in the area, which has everything from creosote to Joshua trees. The park is located off Highway 14 just north of Mojave, California (PO Box 1615, Cantil, California 93519).

THE LIVING DESERT — A 1200-acre preserve dedicated to desert exhibits, with everything from Arabian oryxes to zebras. Located in Palm Desert, California at 47-900 Portola Avenue (619-346-5694).

FURTHER INFORMATION

Barstow Resource Area
150 Coolwater Lane
Barstow, California 92311
619-255-8700

California Desert District Office
6221 Box Springs Boulevard
Riverside, California 92507
909-697-5200

California Department of Parks
   and Recreation
Mojave Desert Sector
1051 West Ave. M, Suite 201
Lancaster, California 93534
805-942-0662

Death Valley National Park
Death Valley, California 92328
619-786-2331

Mojave National Preserve
831 Barstow Road
Barstow, California 92311
619-256-3591

Interagency Visitor Center
Junctions Hwy. 395 and Hwy. 136
Drawer R
Lone Pine, California 93545
619-876-6222

Joshua Tree National Park
74485 National Monument Drive
Twentynine Palms, California 92277
619-367-7511

Needles Resource Area
101 West Spike's Road
PO Box 888
Needles, California 92363
619-326-3896

Providence Mountains State
   Recreation Area
PO Box 1
Essex, California 92332-0001
805-942-0662

II

The Colorado Desert

The sun was now so high, as to beam upon us
with the same insufferable radiance of yesterday.
The air which we inhaled, seemed to scald our
lungs. [My companions] had so completely
abandoned the hope of ever reaching the water
... that they threw themselves on the ground ...
resigned to die. I instantly determined to remain
with my father, be it life or death. To this determination he would by no means consent [and
insisted] that I should go on and [see if there
were] any water at hand ... Imagine my joy [a
little further on] at seeing a clear, beautiful running stream of water, just below us at the foot of
the hill! ... [This region] seemed a more fitting
abode for fiends than any living thing that
belongs to our world. During our passage across
it we saw not a single bird, nor the track of any
quadruped, or in fact, anything that had life ...
This very extensive plain, the Sahara of
California, runs north and south, and is bounded
on each side by high barren mountains, some of
which are covered with perpetual snow.

— James Ohio Pattie,
Personal Narrative (1823)

Borrego Springs fan palm oasis, Anza-Borrego State Park (California)

THE COLORADO DESERT IS A PROVINCE of the Sonoran Desert. Like any province, the Colorado shares many characteristics of the larger region in which it is found, but is distinct enough to be considered a separate entity. Located in Southern California west of the Colorado River, south of the Mojave, and east of the Pacific coastal mountains, this low, hot desert lacks the large upright saguaro and organ pipe cactus that are synonymous with the Sonoran proper, but possesses many other plant species — ocotillo, agave, paloverde — common in southwestern Arizona. Like the Sonoran, the Colorado is a subtropical desert, with a greater number of plant and animal species than the more northerly Mojave, Great Basin, or Painted deserts. A trip to the deserts of Southern California in March or April, after a season of plentiful rainfall, presents an incredible spectacle of nature's vitality — the brilliant colors of the barrel and beavertail cactus flowers, the fresh green growth on wild palm trees, the yellow blossoms of the brittlebush.

We know little of the earliest residents of the Colorado Desert. Here and there a few artifacts remain — rock circles resembling the tepee circles of the Plains Indians, stone grinding tools, potsherds, arrowheads, and scattered bones and basket shreds. We can imagine the first residents found the interior desert a reasonable place to live, without the snow and cold of the high mountains, but lacking in the more abundant resources and mild Mediterranean climate of the Pacific Coast. These early pioneers probably utilized nature's bounty on a seasonal basis, moving as the deer and bighorn moved and as plants matured and produced edible fruits (cactus fruit, wild berries) and seeds (mesquite, acorns). Scientists believe the agave was one of the most important plants in their world, producing food as well as fibers for sandals and bowstrings. Yucca served a similar dual purpose.

By the eighteenth century, the Spanish had been in the New World for over 200 years. Their cities, roads, churches and universities had transformed the physical, spiritual and intellectual landscape of Central and South America. Slowly, their empire began to expand north into what is now the American Southwest. In 1774, Juan Bautista de Anza, commander of a remote outpost in Sonora, decided to search for an overland route to Monterey, an active Spanish port on the northern Pacific Coast. His expedition brought the first Euroamericans into the region known today as the Colorado Desert. Anza crossed into the desert south of the Salton Sea region and then navigated in a northwesterly direction through present-day Imperial County and San Diego County. His route took him just east of Borrego Springs, which currently sits in the center of Anza-Borrego State Park, and then north to the old Spanish road to Monterey. The success of

Scenic Font's Point, Anza-Borrego State Park (California)

Rare desert waterfall after spring rain, Colorado Desert (California)

Anza's mission brought more settlers into the region, where they encoun-
tered an increasingly hostile group of natives.

The first Americans in the region were mountain man James Ohio Pattie
and his father, whose restless wanderings (1824–1827) in the northern
regions of Old Mexico took them across the Colorado Desert, probably
through the Algodones Dunes (see epigraph), and over the coastal range to
San Diego. The American era formally commenced with the conclusion of the
Mexican War and the discovery of gold at Sutter's Mill near Sacramento,
California. The first priority of the new landlords was to scout the area for
possible rail routes. As part of that process, the expedition of Lieutenant
Henry Abbot (1853–1855) undertook a reconnaissance of Southern
California that included the Colorado Desert. Because a route across the
Sierra Nevadas was deemed technologically impossible, the authors of the
Pacific Railroad Survey recommended that the rail line run from Fort Yuma
on the Colorado River across the low desert to the Pacific Coast, a route that
would eventually become occupied by the Southern Pacific Railroad.

A little matter back east known as the Civil War diverted attention from
the railroad projects for nearly a decade. During that time, the famous
Butterfield-Overland mail route plied its dusty way from Tucson in the
Arizona Territories to Los Angeles in the new state of California. This long
and sometimes dangerous route, also known as the Southern Emigrant Trail,

took thousands of
people through the
middle of the Colo-
rado Desert, with
stops at now-historic
sites such as Carriso,
Palm Springs,
Vallecito, San Felipe
and Warner's Ranch.
After the war, a mas-
sive western migra-
tion — Manifest
Destiny — took

Barrel cactus, Colorado Desert (California)

place. Whatever quiet
isolation and anonymity the Colorado Desert had previously enjoyed were
gone forever. A familiar American frontier migration soon followed — sunburned prospectors, rifle-toting cattle ranchers, pioneering homesteaders,
eager merchants, university scientists with collecting boxes and Latin binomi-
als, curious cross-country visitors and, finally, gas stations and air-conditioned cabins to support a burgeoning tourist industry. In 1933, the

Pencil cholla, Anza-Borrego State Park (California)

farsighted people of California established the Anza-Borrego Desert State Park. Today, over a million visitors a year are attracted to the park.

The California fan palm is the plant I most associate with the Colorado Desert. You can find them in a variety of places, but they are most easily seen at the end of the trail in Borrego Canyon, through which a nice little stream runs in the spring. The larger palms stand sixty feet tall, with thick crowns of five-foot fronds. As the palm fronds die they collapse downwards on the trunk. On some of the trees these dead, brown leaves form a skirt that reaches nearly to the ground. There are many nice views of the palms, but the best is on your back, looking upward. This is the view of the desert tortoise, the coyote, the rattlesnake. From that perspective you can fully appreciate the pillar-like stature of the tree, the exotic richness of the crown, the symmetry of the split green fronds against the deep blue sky. The leaves are slightly varnished, so they produce a shimmering mirror-like effect in the breeze. In short, a wonderful surprise of a tree to find in the middle of a parched desert.

In the same area of Borrego Canyon you will see, in a good year, the incredible scarlet blossoms of the ocotillo, like burning flames at the end of each green, wand-like stalk. Other common cactuses in the area include the cholla, the beavertail, and the barrel. Brittlebush is thick in Borrego Canyon and, again in a good year, you will be treated to a wonderful display of sulphur-yellow flowers.

Ironwood trees are one of the most peculiar residents of the Anza-Borrego country. These unusual trees, which stand about 30 feet high, produce white blossoms in June but for the rest of the year are bare. You can find them at Yaqui Well in San Felipe Wash and at Tamarisk Grove Campground. Also found here is the elephant tree, so named because of its swollen trunk, tentacle-like branches, and a blood-like sap — like something from Ovid's *Metamorphoses* — and more common to Mexico than to the United States. The bizarre trees can be seen on a trail near the Elephant Trees Ranger Station on Split Mountain Road.

The animals seen most often in the Colorado Desert (which includes the

Close-up of Teddy bear cholla, Colorado Desert (California)

Ocotillo and brittlebush, Colorado Desert (California)

southernmost parts of Joshua Tree National Park) are the small ones —
horned lizards, desert iguanas, collared lizards, chuckwallas, kangaroo rats,
rabbits, and sidewinders. Coyotes, deer, and ringtails are less frequently
seen, with the best chances at dusk and dawn. Birding can be good in some
of the canyons, such as Borrego Canyon and Coyote Canyon. If you are
very fortunate, you will see one of the elusive desert bighorn sheep in
Borrego Canyon. Always be alert for mountain lions in Anza-Borrego.
While hiking, look back down the trail every so often. It is also a good idea
to hike in groups of two or more, and, of course, never leave children out of
sight or unattended in mountain lion country.

In the end, the Colorado Desert is most amazing not so much for what
it is as for where it is located. Standing at Font's Point, looking out over vast,
uninhabited Carrizo Badlands, or huffing and puffing up a lonely side-ridge
in Borrego Canyon, it is difficult to believe that you are within a two hour
drive of over 20 million people. If you have time to visit just one desert type
in North America, the Colorado may be the one. Easily accessible from Los
Angeles and San Diego, the Colorado Desert offers many of our most beautiful cactuses, cool green oases of California fan palm, and some of the most
fascinating geology in North America.

PALMS AND PALOVERDES:
ANZA-BORREGO DESERT STATE PARK

This is the country of cactus and mesquite and creosote bush.
Hotter in summer, warmer in winter, than the higher parts, it is the
region most properly called desert country.

—Joseph Wood Krutch
The Desert Year

GETTING THERE

Most people travel to **Anza-Borrego** from the California coast, via Interstate 15. Turn east at the Escondido exit north of San Diego, and take State Route 78 over the coastal mountains (Cleveland National Forest) into the heart of Anza-Borrego. It is about a 50-mile drive on a winding mountain road from Escondido to the state park.

Anza-Borrego is the largest state park west of the Mississippi, and rivals its distant eastern cousin, Adirondack State Park, for diversity of habitats, spectacular natural beauty, and inaccessible wild country. Just 90 minutes east of San Diego, Anza-Borrego is truly another world, a country ruled from dusk to dawn by the desert sun, and through the night by the tiny elf owl and the tawny mountain lion. The park comprises over 600,000 acres, which puts it on the order of Rhode Island in size. Over 1,000 plant species are found in Anza-Borrego, which protects habitats ranging from dry alkali lakes to pine-covered mountains. In recent years, the park has become increasingly popular with Europeans, who fly half-way around the world to marvel at the eerily beautiful badlands, the palm-filled oases, the bizarre elephant trees, the distant vistas of the Salton Sea, the deeply eroded canyons, and numerous historic sites. It may be snowing and thirty below in January at Jackson Hole, Wyoming, but January in Anza-Borrego can see sunny skies and temperatures hovering around eighty.

 POINTS OF INTEREST

BORREGO SPRINGS CANYON — One of the most popular trails in Southern California, the well-traveled Borrego Canyon trail provides a short (3 miles round trip) and informative walk through the Colorado Desert. At peak season (spring), be prepared for crowds on this trail. Best to leave early. The self-guided nature walk will introduce you to alluvial fans, wild ocotillo and brittlebush gardens, dry washes, morteros and metates (rock depressions made by Cahuilla Indians from grinding seeds), desert varnish (a dark patina on desert rocks), honey mesquite (nutritious beans), creosote and catclaw patches, and the habitat of the endangered Peninsula bighorn sheep. At the end of the trail is a lush grove of California fan palms, one of 25 native groves found in Anza-Borrego. In years of heavy spring rains, there is also a nice waterfall on the intermittent stream before the grove.

COYOTE CANYON — Coyote Canyon, located in the northwestern portion of the park, is an excellent place for day hiking and wildlife observation. The canyon is unique because of its year-round stream. This is along the route of the 1774 Anza expedition, which included 240 settlers and nearly 1,000 head of livestock. Anza went on to form the village that is today perhaps the most beautiful city in North America, San Francisco. In this canyon you are literally walking in the footsteps of California and American history.

ELEPHANT TREES TRAIL — This self-guided nature trail begins off Split Mountain Road south of Ocotillo Wells on Highway 78. Although the trail is designed primarily to introduce you to the elephant tree, you will also see patches of indigo bush and barrel cactus, smoke tree and desert lavender, catclaw, and buckhorn cholla.

EROSION ROAD — This self-guided auto tour along County Road S-22 takes you through some classic features of the Colorado Desert. You will see the remnants of a playa (or extinct lake), in which shrimp still exist via drought-resistant eggs; alluvial fans; Font's Point; the San Jacinto Fault; the Borrego Badlands; and the distant Salton Sea, which was filled in 1905 after irrigation canals ruptured and filled the playa with water for over a year.

FONT'S POINT — Famous for its view of the Borrego Badlands, Font's Point is reached via a sandy four-mile track, which at times can be navigated only by four-wheel-drive vehicles. The view is awesome at sunrise and sunset. Twenty thousand years ago there was a grassy savanna and a large fresh-water lake below the highlands. Paleontologists have unearthed numerous fossils in the badlands and elsewhere in the park — everything from corals etched in dusty limestone to heavy mammoth bones bound in ancient clay.

Sidewinder, Colorado Desert (California).   Photo courtesy of U.S. Fish and Wildlife Service (California)

NARROWS EARTH TRAIL — A valuable and educational walk for those interested in geology, this self-guided trail is located east of the Tamarisk Grove Campground on Highway 78. Here you will see crystalline igneous rock associated with earlier periods of mountain formation, sedimentary layers formed under water ages ago, metamorphic rocks created by intense heat and pressure, and the effects of differential erosion, faulting, and alluvial processes.

SOUTHERN EMIGRANT TRAIL — This is a self-guided auto tour that follows the historic route of the Southern Emigrant Trail through the park. Along the way you will see the San Felipe Stage Station (formerly an Indian village), Walker Pass, Box Canyon, the Vallecito Stage Station (see below), and Palm Spring, another stop on the Butterfield-Overland stage route, which, incredibly, ran from Tipton, Missouri over 2,000 miles to San Francisco (the trip required 24 bone-jarring days).

SPLIT MOUNTAIN — Like the Narrows Earth Trail, Split Mountain provides living instruction in the processes of geomorphology. The mountain was literally split in two by earthquakes and the erosive effects of flash floods. Reached via Split Mountain Road south of the turn-off to Elephant Trees Nature Trail.

OTHER SITES

ALGODONES DUNES — Along Interstate 8, about 15 miles west of Yuma, Arizona, there is a pull-off and parking area where travelers can hike among the Algodones Dunes. Spring wildflower displays can be impressive in this area, particularly after a wet winter. This is most likely James Ohio Pattie's "Sahara of California."

IMPERIAL NATIONAL WILDLIFE REFUGE — For 30 miles on either side of the Colorado River, the Imperial refuge protects desert lowlands and uplands. In winter, large flocks of geese utilize the riparian areas. A popular place for fishing and hunting, as well as less disruptive photography and wildlife observation. Access is from Yuma, Arizona.

VALLECITO STAGE STATION COUNTY PARK — Located south of the Vallecito Mountains and adjacent to Anza-Borrego State Park, this San Diego County park preserves a stage stop and historic cemetery on the old Southern Emigrant Trail between St. Louis and San Francisco. The stage station was built in 1852. Access is from the Ocotillo exit on Interstate 8, via Highway 2.

FURTHER INFORMATION

Manager
Imperial National Wildlife Refuge
Box 1032
Yuma, Arizona 85364

Superintendent
Anza-Borrego Desert State Park
Borrego Springs, California 92004
619-767-3052/4684
Camping reservations may be made at 800-444-7275.

III

The Sonoran Desert

On the mountains and the mesas the saguaro is
so common that perhaps we overlook its beauty
of form; yet its lines are sinuous as those of a
Moslem minaret, its fluting as perfect as those of
a Doric column. Often you see it standing on a
ledge of some rocky peak, like the long shaft of
a ruined temple on a Greek headland.

—John C. Van Dyke,
from *The Desert*

LARGE CACTUSES, AS VAN DYKE INDICATES, are synonymous with
the Sonoran Desert. The lofty saguaro. The lovely organ pipe. The fat fleshy
barrel. The names are familiar, even as the distinctive forms, for their silhou-
ettes have been captured in a million photographs and post cards, wall calen-
dars and Christmas cards, frozen in time against the famous red Arizona
sunset. The Sonoran is an exotic desert, quite unlike other deserts of the
United States, for it is a desert with cactuses the size of trees. An arboreal
desert. In places this unique subtropical desert resembles the East African
lowlands — coastal Tanzania and Kenya. One almost expects to see a black-
horned gazelle nibbling on a green acacia in a dry wash, or a pride of red-
faced, yawning lions scattered about the carcass of a wildebeest near a palm
spring. It has that unfamiliar, *magical* look about it. In the end, though, the
Sonoran is what it is: an American desert, a temporally recent (the geographers tell us) desert, a complex community of plants and animals that have
evolved over time and space together — the mountain lion superintending
the mule deer, the rattlesnake overseeing the rodents, the butterflies pollinat-

Organ pipe cactus, Sonoran Desert (Arizona)

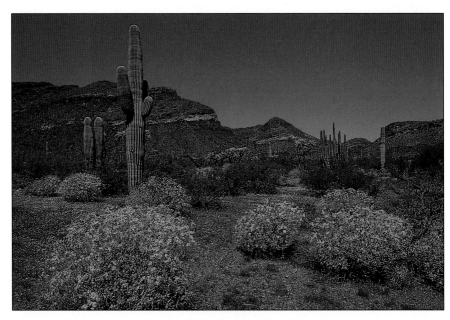

Saguaro and organ pipe cactus, Organ Pipe Cactus National Monument (Arizona)

ing the cactuses. All for no other purpose than to capture the light of the sun, move it through the plants into the animals, and facilitate the reproductive needs of both. Or so some say.

Historians tell us *Homo sapiens* has long left footprints on the sands of southwestern Arizona. Exactly when the first inhabitants arrived is a source of lively conversation among experts. Some place the date at around 15,000 years ago. Others, citing radiocarbon data, push the figure back to two times that, or more. This much we can state with confidence. By around 300 B.C., the Hohokam had begun to encounter some success in the Gila and Salt River valleys. These folks would go on to build extensive irrigation canals, sturdy stone houses and flourishing villages, beautiful pottery, jewelry, and other cultural artifacts. They would reached their zenith around A.D. 800 and then, following the path of everything in nature, from fields of grass to spiral galaxies, their way of life would begin to decline, with the last act occurring sometime in the fifteenth century.

Traditionally, a large portion of the Sonoran Desert was the homeland of the Papago and Pima Indians, tribes whose members still inhabit southern Arizona. Over the border in Mexico, in the vicinity of the Rio Sonora, there were Seri Indians. Toward the north and east of Tucson lived the Apache. In 1539, Franciscan Father Marcos de Liza wandered through the Sonoran

Desert searching for the Seven Cities of Cibola. The following year the New World Spanish entered the area in force, when the expedition of Coronado proceeded north from Sonora through the neighborhood of present-day Tucson. By the seventeenth century, Spanish

Ocotillo blossom, Sonoran Desert (Arizona)

settlements, presidios, churches, mines, and ranches were liberally sprinkled across the Sonoran Desert at such locations as Tucson, Tubac, Santa Cruz, Fronteras, and Bacoachi (last three in contemporary Sonora). It was not long before the Spanish found themselves in conflict with the Apache, a state of affairs that persisted almost to the twentieth century. In some cases, Apache uprisings compelled the abandonment of all but Tucson and Tubac.

Americans were late coming to the Sonoran country. The first arrival was the occasional trapper and incorrigible wanderer, James Ohio Pattie, who with his father, entered the territory in 1825 en route to further adventures in Sonora and Chihuahua. Later, American explorer David Jackson (a colleague of Jedediah Smith) traveled from Sante Fe to California in 1832, following the old Spanish trading routes through Tucson, the Gila River and eventually the Colorado and Mojave deserts. The conclusion of the Mexican War in 1848 brought Arizona into the Union as a territory. Six years later, the $10 million Gadsen Purchase put another 30,000 square miles under the American flag. The

Yellow brittlebush, Sonoran Desert, looking south into Old Mexico (Arizona)

rest of the century consisted of steady American expansion across the region, a voracious amoeba known as Manifest Destiny.

The best known historical figure of Sonoran country in the nineteenth century was Cochise, a Chiricahua Apache chieftain who maintained his stronghold in the Dragoon Mountains about 50 miles east of Tucson. Who among us over the age of forty can forget the movie *Broken Arrow* (or the 1950s television series by the same name), which dramatized the unlikely friendship between Cochise and postmaster Tom Jeffords (played by Jimmy Stewart)? Cochise's homeland ranged from the Chiricahua Mountains west to the vicinity of Tucson and Tubac, and south 80 miles into Sonora, including the Mexican presidio at Fronteras and the towns of Magdalena on the Rio Magdalena and Arispe on the Rio Sonora. It was a vast territory, and ultimately proved impossible to defend against the persistent assaults, and insults, of Euroamerican civilization.

Cochise's name derived from the Apache *co-cheis*, meaning "like or strong as an oak." By his early twenties, the man stood six feet tall, with long black hair, broad shoulders, thick chest, roman nose, and what one army officer described as a "handsome face" with a "kindly, almost melancholy" expression. In time his character proved true to his name, for Cochise developed into one of the most influential leaders in the Old Southwest. The turning point in his relations with the Americans occurred in February, 1861, when three of his relatives were killed at Fort Bowie in a dispute over some stolen cattle and a captured boy. From this point forward, a state of war existed between the Chiricahua and the Americans, as it had already for two centuries between the Chiricahua and the Mexicans. After suffering defeat at the Battle of Apache Pass on July 16, 1862, Cochise and the other Apache chieftains returned to their time-honored guerrilla tactics, which consisted of carefully planned ambushes and simultaneous raids designed to confuse the enemy. With a band of only 300 warriors, Cochise successfully created fear and uncertainty over 10,000 square miles for nearly a decade.

In the early 1870s, however, Cochise began to tire of war and, perhaps sensing his own mortality, expressed concern for the ultimate fate of his people. At a meeting with General Gordon Granger in 1871, he spoke of his desire for peace:

> *I have come with my hands open to you to live in peace with you. I speak straight and do not wish to deceive or be deceived. I want a good, strong and lasting peace ... Now that I am to speak, the sun, the moon, the earth, the air, the waters, the birds and beasts, even the children unborn shall rejoice at my words. The white*

people have looked for me long. I am here!... I am no longer chief of all the Apaches. I am no longer rich; I am but a poor man. The world was not always this way. God made us not as you; we were born like the animals, in the dry grass, not on beds like you. This is why we do as the animals, go about at night and rob and steal. If I had such things as you have, I would not do as I do, for then I would not need to do so. There are Indians who go about killing and robbing. I do not command them. If I did they would not do so... When I was young I walked all over this country, east and west, and saw no other people than the Apaches. After many summers I walked again and found another race of people had come to take it. How is it?... When I was going around the world, all were asking for Cochise. Now he is here — you see him and hear him — are you glad? If so, say so. Speak, Americans and Mexicans, I do not wish to hide anything from you nor have you hide anything from me. I will not lie to you. Do not lie to me.

Although peace with Granger proved impossible to attain, Cochise soon consummated a treaty with General Oliver Otis Howard, a one-armed Civil War veteran and Medal of Honor winner who later founded Howard University for African-Americans in Washington, D.C. Howard's visit to the stronghold was facilitated by Cochise's friend, Tom Jeffords, who had previously struck an agreement with Cochise on the safe passage of civilian mail over the Apache homeland. As part of their agreement, Cochise insisted that Jeffords be appointed commissioner of the new Chiricahua reservation in southeastern Arizona.

Three years later, Cochise became seriously ill and realized he was going to die. He called for his friend Tom Jeffords, and the following conversation is reported to have occurred:

Cochise asked [of Jeffords]: "Do you think you will see me alive again?"

Jeffords replied: "No, I do not think I will."

"I think I will die about ten o'clock tomorrow morning. Do you think we will see each other again?"

Jeffords was silent for a moment. "I don't know. What do you think about it?"

"I have been thinking a good deal about it while I have been sick here, and I believe we will: good friends will meet again — up there [pointing to the sky]."

Hedgehog cactus in blossom, Sonoran Desert (Arizona)

Cochise died at the time predicted and was shortly buried, along with his best horse and favorite dog, in a rock fissure of the Dragoon Mountains. Jeffords was present at the burial and never revealed the location of the grave to any white man. Twelve years after Cochise's death, Geronimo and Cochise's son, Naiche, surrendered to General Nelson Miles. They spent the rest of their lives in Florida and Oklahoma. Today, the Chiricahua Apache have no reservation of their own. They live among other Indians on reservations in New Mexico and Arizona. Cochise loved and understood the desert lands in ways we will never know, and fought for their freedom with a passion that even his worst enemies respected. Buried deep in the mountains of his desert stronghold, he is part of them forever.

Arizona achieved statehood in 1912. Since then we have had the customary sequence of events: large ancestral ranches and farms dominating the hinterlands, the gradual disappearance of livestock killers such as coyotes and mountain lions, grotesquely burgeoning urban areas, a substantial military presence, escalating conflicts with endangered species, a gradual shift of political power from the country to the city, loss of water both above ground and below ground, and, finally, the arrival of various curious artists, photographers and literary types. Through it all, the Sonoran Desert has endured, protected in places by parks and refuges, in other areas being slowly dismembered, cactus by cactus, tortoise by tortoise, bighorn by bighorn, acre by subdivided acre.

When I think of the Sonoran Desert I think most of the plants. It is an arboreal desert — cactuses of tree-like dimensions — but more than that it is a desert of great floral diversity. This is particularly evident in the spring

Magnificent saguaro cactus, Sonoran Desert (Arizona)

Owl's ears in blossom on desert floor, Sonoran Desert (Arizona)

(March and April) when, given a period of sufficient rainfall, the desert blossoms with spectacular vitality. In fact, the Sonoran Desert has more plant and animal species than the other desert provinces of North America. Why? The short answer is that the area has rainfall in both the winter and summer months. High mountains also help, capturing the clouds that rain down their flanks and fill the springs and, sometimes, the parched streambeds.

My favorite tree in the Sonoran Desert is the paloverde. In Spanish *paloverde* means "green stick" — the paloverde has green chlorophyll in its trunk and branches. The leaves are so small as to be an afterthought. If the country dries up, the tree sheds the leaves like so many worthless relatives. It can afford to — the primary location of photosynthesis is in the trunk and the branches. The paloverde is best seen in early April when the branches are covered with masses of vibrant yellow flowers. Put a wind behind the tree, and stretch a deep blue Arizona sky above, and there are few more magnificent celebrations of the equinox in North America.

The saguaro is another marvel of this desert, a huge columnar cactus with arms that twist and turn into human-like shapes (or is it that humans assume saguaro forms?). This cactus tree is a miracle of adaption, reaching to 50 feet in height and living as long as 200 years. To walk in a "forest" of these giant cactuses on a day when the thermometer has climbed over 100 degrees and the ground is bone dry, is to experience the essence of the paradox of the riddle of the desert — how so much life can flourish in such a frugal, even brutal environment. To add to the odds against it, the flowers of the saguaro remain open only for one night and one day. In that brief time they must be pollinated by a bird, a bat, or a butterfly. Months later, if successful, the saguaro produce a red fruit. The Papago not only ate the fruit, they also fermented it in order to produce a tasty beverage.

A whole cast of colorful and comedic animal characters inhabit the cactus country of southern Arizona. The coatimundi is one of the most bizarre, an animal apparently designed when its creator was slightly drunk, with a long pointed nose, fluffy slightly prehensile tail and ridiculous lumbering gait, a shuffling mixture of spider monkey, opposum and house cat. What makes it even more improbable is that the coati, or chullu, travels in wandering troupes, the bands presenting the appearance of an itinerant group of vaudevilleans in search of a vacant theater. Where the coatimundi seems put on the landscape to amuse, the diamondback rattlesnake is all business, a cold-blooded viper straight from the brain of Edgar Allen Poe, the ultimate midnight terror to whole nations of warm-blooded rodents. If you are out hiking in the desert in July and August and see a large number of nine or ten inch rattlers, beware. You are near a nest, and the mother may still be

Red ocotillo, Organ Pipe Cactus National Monument (Arizona)

Paloverde tree in early spring, Sonoran Desert (Arizona)

around. But leave them be, for without rattlesnakes, coral snakes, and copperheads, the desert would be crawling with pocket mice, ground squirrels and kangaroo rats — all carriers of disease and vermin. There are so many others out there that could be added to the census — bobcats and bullfrogs, badgers and bats, elf owls (the world's smallest) and golden eagles, peccaries and pronghorns, skunks and sheep. In days gone by, there were jaguars too, and Mexican wolves. In days gone by. Each animal, like each person, must contend with the circumstances into which it is born. In the case of the Sonoran, these organisms find themselves in a very hard world. Just getting a drink of water can be a difficult and dangerous undertaking. But somehow they do it, year after year, generation after generation. I salute them all. They deserve our respect and our assistance, insofar as many of them only endure at this point through human generosity.

No one (at least no one I know) can walk the Sonoran Desert and not be changed. There is a natural power here that uplifts even as it humbles: the panoramic shimmering views deep into Old Mexico on clear sunny days, the Milky Way stretched like a giant luminous trail across the night sky, the lovely white flowers of the saguaro turning pink in the first light of dawn. This is the historic cactus desert of Cochise and Jeffords, the mythic wild frontier of John Wayne and Clint Eastwood, the serene literary landscape of Joseph Wood Kruth and Edward Abbey. It is a desert on the actual and figurative border, sprawling hundreds of miles south into Baja and Sonora, comprehending whole provinces of the imagination and spirit. It is a desert that straddles two countries and is claimed by both, but owes allegiance to neither. It is a desert that once attracted eccentric prospectors and hard-rock miners, and now lures men, women and children with cameras and tripods, tape recorders and bird guides. It is, in short, a good country, an excellent land, famous around the world, and we are fortunate to have it so close to where we live.

CACTUS PARADISE:
ORGAN PIPE CACTUS
NATIONAL MONUMENT

There's something about the desert that doesn't like man,
something that mocks his nesting instinct and makes his
constructions look feeble and temporary. Yet it's just that
inhospitableness that endears the arid rockiness, the places
pointy and poisonous, to men looking for its discipline.
— William Least Heat Moon, *Blue Highways*

You approach from the north, through Ajo (home of the gargantuan
open-pit copper mine), and the little crossroads of Why (why not?), and then
you turn right down a long dry stretch of blacktop. If it is July or August,
you have the road all to yourself. If it is in the period from October to April,
you will have company. Lots
of it. Retired orthodontists
piloting RVs the size of eigh-
teen-wheelers. Motorcycles
with side cars, both occupants
over 70 years old. Red
Corvettes driven by little old
ladies from Pasadena. And so
on. Organ Pipe, and the
Mexican country beyond, are
the winter demesne of the
snowbirds, the retired folk
who migrate, from Arizona to
Alaska, as the seasons and
their desires dictate. They are
wonderful people, excellent
stewards and warm and
friendly comrades in the
campground. I love them all.

Organ Pipe is one of the
monuments at which desert
rat Edward Abbey worked
during his younger years (early
40s). I suppose work is the
word for it. From his journals,

Desert pavement, with hedgehog cactus in blossom,
Sonoran Desert (Arizona)

Close-up of saguaro cactus, Saguaro National Park (Arizona)

it sounds like Old Ed spend most of his time on "patrol" in the back country, which for Abbey meant wandering all over the place on foot or in a park vehicle, doing what he would be doing even if he wasn't in park uniform. In any event, Organ Pipe is, as Abbey wrote, a nature-lover's paradise. Although there aren't as many developed trails as in other parks, most hiking is by line of sight, as there are no woods to become lost in. Organ Pipe has over 330,000 acres, making it larger than either Rocky Mountain or Grand Teton national parks.

GETTING THERE

To reach **Organ Pipe** from Tucson, take exit 99 on Interstate 19 in the heart of town. Drive west on Ajo Way or State 86 for 115 miles to Why, Arizona. Turn south at Why on State 86. Within a few miles you'll be in beautiful Organ Pipe.

In olden days, the area known as Organ Pipe Cactus National Monument was regularly traversed by a hundred generations of Indians and, later, by sun-darkened Spanish soldiers and kindly Jesuit missionaries. The early explorer Diaz passed through here, as did Father Kino, who set up a little adobe mission at Sonoyta over the border. Such places at Quitobaquito Springs and Mount Ajo were well known to these antiquarian folk, as they were to the native Papago Indians (who now reside on a large reservation east of the monument). Later, grizzled prospectors and cattlemen called this country home, as well as corporate miners (as can be seen at Ajo and elsewhere).

Since 1937, when the national monument was established by a man (FDR) in the White House whose idea of nature was Warm Springs, Georgia, the chief attraction of the Ajo Mountains, Bates Mountains and Puerto Blanco Mountains has been the tall (nearly 20-foot), multi-trunked organ pipe cactus, a green marvel of nature well adapted to life in this dry region. Like much of what lives in southern Arizona, the organism is happier in Mexico, where frost is rare. For that reason, you will find the organ pipe primarily on south-facing slopes, facing the motherland, an exposure where the sun comes early and leaves late and warms the rock with a heat that lingers awhile into the night. Like the saguaro, the organ pipe has the ability to store water, a process that swells its pleated skin in times of plenty, and leaves the ridged stems shrunken but alive in times of drought. Interestingly, the organ pipe opens its fragrant blossoms, a beautiful lavender-white, only at night when pollination by bats and moths is accomplished.

Organ Pipe is a place to visit in the dead of winter, when the snow has drifted over the driveway, the firewood supply is getting low, and you simply cannot watch another football game. It is a place of deep blue skies and warm sun and singing cactus wrens. A place where you can take a walk on New Year's Day and not worry about insulated boots, fur-fringed parkas, or frostbite. A place to come to when you are cold of body and weary of spirit and need to be rejuvenated. If you are lucky, you will see a finely sculpted white-tail deer silhouetted against the sky, or a nearsighted javelina grunting down a paloverde wash, or a beaded black-and-gold gila monster ambling across the pavement. Even if you only see a harvester ant you will still have beheld a miracle. Organ Pipe is a friendly and forgiving land, in winter, when the summer heat is just a memory and the rains have stirred the expectations of desert green. It is a land full of hope and faith and good cheer. Some people have therapists, medication regimes, behavioralists, weekly groups and twelve-step programs. Others have places like Organ Pipe.

 ## POINTS OF INTEREST

AJO MOUNTAIN DRIVE — This fairly good dirt road, one of two popular scenic drives in the park, begins near the Visitor Center and leads 21 miles through the foothills of the major mountain range in the park. Wildflower displays along this route in the spring can be magnificent, and many famous pictures by such masters as David Muench and

Jeff Gnasse have been taken here. Also, there are some spectacular assemblages of organ pipe and saguaro cactus, all set with the spectacular peaks and crags of the Ajo Mountains in the background. This area was actively used by local Indians during the period from about 7,000 B.C. to the second century A.D.

ALAMO CANYON — A popular day hiking area, Alamo Canyon is located north of the Visitor's Center about 10 miles on Highway 85. The dirt access road is on the east side of Highway 85 just north of the Diablo Mountains.

BULL CANYON TRAIL — The Bull Canyon trail begins at the Estes Canyon Picnic Area on Ajo Mountain Drive. This is about halfway along the 21-mile, one-way road. There are two approaches to Bull Canyon — the direct route to the south, and the loop route through Estes Canyon. Either approach of about four miles round trip will lead you through communities of mixed cactus and paloverde, and jojoba and evergreen, all in the shadow of Mount Ajo (4808 feet). Look for *tinajas*, natural depressions in the rock that hold rainwater for desert wildlife.

PALOVERDE TRAIL — This 1.3 mile trail connects the campground and the visitor center and provides excellent views of the jagged Ajo Mountains, especially at sunset.

PUERTO BLANCO DRIVE — Like the Ajo Mountain Drive, this long primitive road leads deep into the Organ Pipe backcountry and provides a chance for folks to experience the Sonoran Desert up close. The dirt road is 53 miles long. Top speeds are five to ten miles an hour, so expect this tour to take at least four or five hours, more if you plan to stop and have a picnic or walk around (highly recommended). You will see it all here — typical desert shrubland composed of paloverde, brittlebush, ocotillo and the smaller cactuses; great stands with hundreds of giant saguaro and organ pipe; the aftereffects of ancient volcanic explosions; geographic features such as dry washes, arroyos, and bajadas; the remnants of Charlie Bell's gold mine; the old Bonita well once used for watering cattle; dry creosote flats; rare elephant trees; and the beautiful Quitobaquito Oasis. I strongly recommend this drive, which is suitable for passenger cars if you drive very slowly and carefully.

QUITOBAQUITO SPRINGS — This is a site that simply must be seen

A beautiful saguaro cactus, Cabeza Prieta National Wildlife Refuge (Arizona)

— a rare, springfed oasis of cottonwoods and cattails on the Puerto Blanco Road about 15 miles west of Highway 85 and just north of the international boundary.

VICTORIA MINE TRAIL — Accessed by a trailhead near the campground (rangers can point the way), this pleasant 2.25 mile hike leads to a former gold and silver mine, an historic relict that evokes a scene from *The Treasure of the Sierra Madre.*

VISITOR CENTER NATURE TRAIL — This is a great little walk, beginning right at the parking lot, and one that will help new visitors learn correct identification of typical Sonoran Desert plants. You will see giant saguaro cactus, paloverde, creosote, cholla, ocotillo, prickly pear, and barrel. Don't poke around the burrows, which may harbor such nocturnal dwellers as tarantulas, scorpions, centipedes and rattlesnakes. Annual rainfall, we learn here, averages about nine inches, with lows recorded of seven inches and highs of 17 inches. Also, the daily highs from mid-June through mid-September can reach 112 degrees Fahrenheit, with surface temperatures nearing 170 degrees Fahrenheit. Not a place to visit on the Fourth of July.

A Mojave rattlesnake in the Sonoran Desert   Photo courtesy of U.S. Fish and Wildlife Service

BRITTLEBUSH AND BIGHORNS:
CABEZA PRIETA
NATIONAL WILDLIFE REFUGE

It's all a great country.
— Doug Peacock,
Counting Sheep

GETTING THERE

The **Cabeza Prieta** Visitor's
Center is located 13 miles
west of Why, Arizona (see
directions for Organ Pipe) on
State Route 85, and just north
of Ajo, Arizona. It is located
on the west side of the road.
Ajo can also be accessed
from the north by exiting
from Interstate 8 at Gila
Bend, Arizona, and driving
south for 40 miles on State
Route 85.

Cabeza Prieta is a vast, wild expanse of
Sonoran Desert that straddles the
U.S./Mexico border about two hours west of
Tucson, Arizona. Early explorers referred to
the path through this area as *El Camino del
Diablo*, the Devil's Highway, a place name
that says much about the country. The
860,000 acre federal wildlife refuge was
formed in 1939 primarily to protect habitat
for the rare desert bighorn sheep. Since World
War II much of the area, which adjoins the
Barry Goldwater Air Force Range, has been
used as a gunnery and aerial bombing range.
As a result, all visitors must stop at refuge
headquarters in Ajo and sign a "Military Hold

Harmless Agreement" as well as obtain a refuge entry permit. Four-wheel drive vehicles are required for the primitive roads (more like trails) in the refuge. This vehicle requirement, together with most people's understandable reluctance to enter a live-fire area with unexploded ordinance, limits visitors to less than 1000 per year (mid-1990s). That is an incredible (and encouraging) figure in this day and age for so vast an area. Cabeza is definitely not a place for the casual visitor, the ill-equipped, or the climatically faint-hearted. Given the poor state of its roads and lack of developed water sites, Cabeza is a big, hot, dangerous desert best suited for only the most experienced naturalists and hikers.

A ring-tailed cat, Sonoran Desert
Photo courtesy of Saguaro National Park

The refuge is named for Cabeza Prieta (Spanish for "Black Head"), a distinctive lava-topped peak in one of its six mountain ranges. The peak is in the west end of the refuge, where there can be less than two inches of annual rainfall. Cabeza is not, despite its reputation, a barren wasteland. With two periods of rainfall (winter and summer), the desert vegetation in places is surprisingly lush, particularly on the eastern bajadas, mountains, and dry washes. Spring is probably the best time to visit Cabeza, especially after a wet winter when the cactuses and plants are fully charged and produce rich flower displays. The yellow brittlebush normally peaks in March, with the smaller cactus flowers coming shortly after. Paloverdes, luminous with light green leaves, can be particularly striking at this time of the year. Saguaro will blossom as late as June. As in other desert communities, the best time for wildlife observation is dawn and dusk. Again, spring is an excellent time, as the songbirds are plentiful, the reptiles are active, and the larger animals such as Sonoran pronghorn and desert bighorn may be visible with their young.

Many visitors choose to park their cars north of Ajo on Charlie Bell Pass Road, and walk into the refuge along the road for several miles. This is an opportunity to see the Sonoran Desert in much less crowded conditions than at Saguaro National Park in Tucson or Organ Pipe National Monument just to the south. Refuge personnel will provide you with a map of this area, the required permits, and instructions for making your visit pleasant and safe. The road twists and turns past Little Tule Well and over Pack Rat Hill before finally climbing up Charlie Bell Pass in the Growler Mountains. Total distance from the refuge boundary to Charlie Bell Pass is about 12 miles one way, so this is not a trip to be undertaken without sufficient water, a good map and compass, and adequate gear and preparation. Someone in good shape, with plenty of water, could make the round-trip hike in one day if it was not a terribly hot day, but there would not be much time for enjoying the scenery along the way. A better idea for most would be to hike in several miles on the road and spend the day in a smaller area, fully savoring its rich offering of desert flora and fauna. It's always fun to take a camera along on such an excursion, and create your own record of the fauna and flora — just stay away from anything that rattles.

The rest of Cabeza will probably always remain a vast and little-visited blank spot on the map, an immense wilderness into which famous desert rats like Ed Abbey and Doug Peacock can disappear, in the bold manner of Jedediah Smith, and rediscover the joy of crossing a little-known country. It is fitting that at least one sizeable portion of the Sonoran Desert north of the border has been set aside as wilderness, in perpetuity, never to be divided

Saguaro cactus growing up through paloverde tree, which acts as a "nurse tree," protecting the cactus in its early years, Organ Pipe Cactus National Monument

with asphalt highways, disfigured with open-pit copper mines, or degraded with strip malls and neon lights. In Cabeza there will forever be a quiet unbroken harmony, the mournful call of the white-winged dove, the lonely wail of the coyote, the bone-chilling cry of the mountain lion, all making a wonderful music that can quiet even the most turbulent heart.

THE CLASSIC LIGHT: SAGUARO NATIONAL PARK

Time has so little meaning in the center of the desert. The land holds a collective memory in the stillness of open spaces. Perhaps our only obligation is to listen and remember.
—Terry Tempest Williams, *All that is Hidden*

Over three million visitors pass through Saguaro National Park each year, one of the few major parks (outside of the Civil War parks) located in the suburbs of a sizeable city. The park, until recently a monument, preserves some unbelievably thick stands of saguaro cactus, interspersed with the standard hedgehog cactus, barrel cactus, cholla, ocotillo and prickly pear. There are actually two Saguaro National Parks. The eastern, and larger unit, is found at the end of Broadway Boulevard in the Rincon Mountains. The western portion, known as the Tucson Mountain District, includes similar terrain and vegetation, and is surrounded by Tucson (a city with a bad case of the sprawls).

For many people, probably most, Saguaro National Park, either east or west, is their first and only close-up view of the true Sonoran Desert. They drive down from Phoenix to escape the urban desert, or fly into Tucson for a convention and get the car for an afternoon, or stop with the family on a cross-country trek. The park is a superb place for that introduction, a natural labora-

GETTING THERE

There are two components to **Saguaro National Park,** and both are located in the environs of Tucson, Arizona. Saguaro West is situated between Picture Rocks Road on the north, Kinney Road on the south, and Sandario Road on the west. To get there, exit Interstate 10 at Ina Road and follow Ina Road west to the Golden Gate Road, which leads south into the park. Saguaro East can be reached via Speedway Boulevard or Broadway Boulevard, both major east-to-west arterials in Tucson. Follow either boulevard east to Freeman Road. Turn south for a few miles to the junction with Old Spanish Trail, where the Visitor Center is located.

tory, lecture hall and library of fascinating Sonoran plants and animals. Chief among those, of course, is the saguaro, which forms the centerpiece for the park, both aesthetically and biologically. Each giant cactus supports a whole community of animals, from insects (honey bees, harvester ants) to various birds. The trunk and arms of the cactus can provide well-protected nesting cavities for such birds as Gila woodpecker, gilded flicker, American kestrel, cactus wren, Lucy's warbler, western kingbird, elf owls, and screech owls. The flowers of the saguaro, a brilliant white, are something to behold in May and June. At that time their sweet nectar attracts everything from longnose bats to honeybees, moths, and even birds. Later, during the summer, the saguaro's pulpy red fruit is treasured by javelinas, coyotes, foxes, and numerous ground-dwelling rodents.

Much of the best hiking in Saguaro is in the eastern portion of the park, known as the Rincon Mountain District. There are about 128 miles of hiking trails in this region. Further, the park backs up into the Rincon Mountain Wilderness Area of Coronado National Forest, which adds another 38,590 acres to the 60,000 wilderness acres of the park. A mixture of BLM and state land to the east expands the desert ecosystem to over 300,000 acres. That is a sizeable chunk of roadless country to get lost in, all within a short bicycle ride of a major city. The area includes several climatic zones, ranging from the cactus country of the desert lowland through a transitional zone of oak and ponderosa woodland, to highland forests of Douglas fir and quaking aspen. Some environmentalists have proposed reintroducing the Mexican wolf into this area.

Two popular trails in the Rincon Mountain District portion of the park are the Tanque Verde Ridge Trail, which leads from the Javalina picnic ground to Tanque Verde Peak (7049 feet), and the Douglas Spring Trail, along the northern border of the park, which can be followed past Douglas Spring to Cow Head Saddle and Chiminea Canyon. All of these are extremely long, all day hikes and, during certain times of the year, you will find quite a bit of company on the trails. But the views at higher elevations are spectacular, and the beauty of the Sonoran Desert, as preserved in this park, is unsurpassed. On the Tucson Mountain District portion of the park, one of the most popular trails is the Hugh Norris Trail to Wasson Peak (4687 feet), which offers a commanding view of the city. As in other parts of the Sonoran, the best time of year for any of these hikes is October to April. Otherwise, be prepared to sweat.

OTHER SITES

ARIZONA STATE MUSEUM — The museum emphasizes archaeology and anthropology, with some fine exhibits of early life in the region. Located in Tucson, on the University of Arizona Campus near the intersection of Park Avenue and University Boulevard (520-621-6302).

ARIZONA-SONORA DESERT MUSEUM — Located on Finney Road in west Tucson, this is one of finest museums of natural history in country. A must see for anyone visiting Tucson, with over 200 animals and 300 types of desert plants (520-883-1380).

CASA GRANDE RUINS NATIONAL MONUMENT — This structure was constructed by the Hohokam people more than 650 years ago. Father Kino saw the ruins and named them in 1694. Located at 110 Ruins Drive in Coolidge, Arizona, south of Phoenix (520-723-3172).

HEARD MUSEUM — This museum, located in Phoenix at 22 East Monte Vista Road, features cultural artifacts from Southwestern Indians (602-252-8848).

KITT PEAK NATIONAL OBSERVATORY — One of the most important research telescopes in the world, this enormous (158-inch) reflector is used to study distant stars and galaxies. The observatory is in the Quinlan Mountains about an hour southwest of Tucson, with access from Highway 86 (520-322-3426).

FURTHER INFORMATION

Cabeza Prieta National Wildlife Refuge
1611 North Second Avenue
Ajo, Arizona 85321
520-387-7742

Organ Pipe National Monument
Route 1, Box 100
Ajo, Arizona 85321
520-387-6849

Saguaro National Park
3693 South Old Spanish Trail
Tucson, Arizona 85730
520-883-6366

IV

The Chihuahuan Desert

We departed the next day, and traversed a ridge seven leagues in width. The stones on it are of scoria and iron. At night we arrived at many houses situated on the banks of a very beautiful river. The masters of them came half way on the road to meet us, carrying their children on their backs. They gave us many little bags of pearl, and of pounded antimony, with which they rub the face. They gave us many beads, and many blankets of cowhide [buffalo robes], and they loaded all that accompanied us with some of everything they had. They eat wild fruit, and the seed of pines. There are in that country small pine trees [pinyon pine], and the cones of them are like small eggs; but the seed is better than those of Castile [Spain], as its husk is very thin, and while green it is beat and made into balls, and thus eaten. If dry, it is, pounded in its husk, and consumed in the form of flour. Those who there received us, after they had touched us went back running to their houses, and directly returned, and did not stop running, going and coming, bringing to us in this manner many things for consumption on the way.

—Alvar Nunez Cabeza da Vaca
Personal Narrative (1529)

THE CHIHUAHUAN DESERT, found in southwestern Texas and southern New Mexico, is a rugged, sunbaked country, a landscape of long dry vistas and stark, pine-speckled mountains. The placenames evoke the diverse natural history and human history of the region: Apache Mountains, Comanche Crossing, Dagger Flat, Dead Horse Mountains, Devil's Lake, Devil Ridge Mountains, Diablo Plateau, Panther Pass, Rattlesnake Mountains, Jornado de Muerto, the Malpais, the Trinity Site. So do the folk figures of the region: the colorful hermit, Bobcat Carter, legendary superheroes Juan Oso and Pecos Bill, world-famous Geronimo, the notorious scalp hunter, John Glanton, the outlaw Billy the Kid and sheriff Pat Garret, the rebel Pancho Villa and his nemesis General Pershing, Judge Roy Bean and the always vigilant Texas Rangers, the adventuresome Augustus McCrae and Captain Call of Larry McMurtry's Pulitzer Prize-winning novel, *Lonesome Dove*. Here is the demesne of the mountain lion and the mule deer, coatimundi and jackrabbit, Gila monster and pocket mouse. Here, in short, is one amazingly rich piece of North America.

Although the geographers tell us that the Chihuahuan Desert is the second largest in North America (Great Basin the largest), only a small portion is found in the United States. The bulk is south of the border, running hundreds of miles along the Sierra Madres to the vicinity of Durango, in the state of Chihuahua. This largely Mexican desert spreads north of the border in only a few places: the region of Big Bend National Park in south Texas, southern New Mexico in the vicinity of Carlsbad and White Sands National Monument, and parts of extreme southeastern Arizona, especially around elevated rock escarpments. The Chihuahuan Desert, like the Mojave, Great Basin, and Painted deserts, is often a desert of the higher elevations, although the winters are not nearly so cold as in those deserts found further north.

Some of the earliest prehistoric sites in North America have been found in and around the Chihuahuan Desert. These suggest *Homo sapiens* has long been a resident of the region. At a time when the ancient Egyptians were just beginning to build the great pyramids, men and women had long occupied the deserts of the lower Rio Grande. They had explored the mountains, crossed the valleys, discovered natural rock strongholds, settled in new homelands, hunted now-extinct animals, harvested nuts and berries, had children, buried their dead, told stories, narrated histories, invented myths. Much of their culture was perishable, and so we have only such artifacts as skulls, bones, flint points, arrowheads, grinding stones, and scattered jewelry from which to paint a picture of their way of life.

More recently, the Chiricahua Apache and Comanche made their homes in the Chihuahuan Desert, living resiliently on an austere and challenging

Lower Rio Grande River, Big Bend National Park, Texas *Photo courtesy of Rick McIntyre*

landscape. Plants such as the yucca and agave were essential to these native tribes, as were wild animals such as the javelina and mule deer. They lived in small to medium-sized bands, and moved about the country in a seasonal fashion, wintering and summering in different locations. The first European

Chisos Mountains, Big Bend National Park, Texas *Photo courtesy of Rick McIntyre*

White Sands National Monument, New Mexico. *Photo courtesy of Rick McIntyre*

contact with these people occurred around 1530, when Spaniard Alvar Nunez Cabeza de Vaca passed through the region, traversing from east to west (his epic journey began — incredible but true — with a shipwreck in Texas). In 1541 the Spanish explorer, Coronado, entered the Chihuahuan

Desert bighorn sheep. *Photo courtesy of Rick McIntyre*

Desert from the south, ultimately following the Rio Grande River into what is now northern New Mexico and southwestern Colorado. Later, the Mexicans colonized the Rio Grande Valley north to Santa Fe, interacting, sometimes violently, with the indigenous pueblo cultures. Mexican religious leaders attempted to moderate the policies of secular officials vis-a-vis the natives, but not always with success. In 1767, the Jesuits were expelled from the New World colonies, primarily for their efforts in this regard.

In the mid-nineteenth century, three events — the Treaty of Gaudalupe Hidalgo following the Mexican War (1846), the discovery of gold in California (1849), and the Gadsen Purchase (1854) — brought Americans en masse into the region. The transcontinental Butterfield Overland Stage route passed through the Chihuahuan Desert in both New Mexico and Texas. Later the Emigrant (or California) Trail followed suit. After the Civil War, American immigration into the area increased tremendously, and brought major conflicts with the native Comanche and Chiricahua Apache. Whereas the Mexicans had for the most part remained along the Rio Grande, following their defensive presidio (firebase) policy, the Americans actively colonized areas deep in the historic homeland of the Apache and Comanche.

A chief figure among the Chiricahua Apache, and probably the best-known person to ever live in the Chihuahuan Desert, was Geronimo, whose amazing biography is known to virtually every schoolchild. The major facts: Geronimo (originally Goyathlay or Gokhlayeh, i.e. "One Who Yawns") was born in a traditional Apache wickiup near the confluence of the West Fork and Middle Fork of the Gila River, in what is now the Gila Wilderness (about 60 miles north of the international border). The year of his birth is uncertain, but was probably in the 1820s. When he was still in his twenties, Geronimo's wife and children were among many killed in a Mexican ambush at Janos, Chihuahua. This event, which occurred while the tribe was assembled to sign a peace treaty, transformed the life of the young medicine man. One year after the massacre in Chihuahua, Geronimo was permitted to lead a retaliatory attack in which both Cochise and Mangas Coloradas played a role. It was there he acquired the name Geronimo, possibly a corruption of "St. Jerome!"

At first friendly to Americans surveying the border (1851) after the Gadsen Purchase — perhaps hoping for a military ally — Geronimo eventually waged war against the new invaders as he had against the Mexicans. This regional war reached its bloody culmination at the Battle of Apache Pass on July 15, 1862, when hundreds of Apache warriors suffered a significant defeat at the hands of U.S. troops near Fort Bowie in the Chiricahua Mountains. Following this incident, Geronimo, as well as other Apache leaders, were in and out of reservations for years, alternately fighting and ceasing hostilities. Many battles and skirmishes were fought in the Chihuahuan Desert and canyons of the Sierra Madre Mountains, where the Apache often took refuge. Geronimo finally surrendered to General Nelson Miles in 1886 near Canyon de los Embudos, Mexico. The rest of his years were spent in Florida and Oklahoma.

President Theodore Roosevelt denied Geronimo's final request, which was to be allowed to see his homeland one last time before he died (1909). Roosevelt may have been more concerned for Geronimo's safety than anything else, as the sons and daughters of the pioneers had long and bitter memories of the territorial struggle (Roosevelt had earlier included Geronimo in his 1901 inaugural procession). To set the record straight for historians, Geronimo dictated an autobiography (1906) that remains in print to this day. There is an old legend in the Southwest, possibly apocryphal, that some time after Geronimo was buried loyal Apache exhumed his remains and placed them in a desert fastness where they would never be disturbed.

The twentieth century has seen major changes in the American part of the Chihuahuan Desert. In 1924, the world's first wilderness area — the Gila — was designated by the federal government in the mountains and canyons of Geronimo's birthplace. This was done largely through the efforts of pioneering conservationist Aldo Leopold, for whom a wilderness area in the Black Range was eventually designated. On July 16, 1945 government scientists involved in the Manhattan Project detonated the world's first atomic bomb at the Trinity Site. Similar bombs were exploded several weeks later over the cities of Hiroshima and Nagasaki, Japan. Later, the 3,260-square-mile White Sands Missile Range was designated as an area for testing German rockets captured in Europe. Technology developed at White Sands soon led to calls for a manned space program.

The area gained national attention in 1947, when an incident occurred near Roswell, New Mexico that is still discussed. Government officials maintain that wreckage recovered in the desert simply consisted of the remnants of a weather balloon, while UFO aficionadoes insist that parts of an alien spacecraft, together with the deceased occupants, were discovered (the incident is a favorite theme of late night cable stations). In 1944, the Big Bend country of southwestern Texas, located in an enormous loop of the Rio Grande River, was designated Big Bend National Park. The fragile desert area had been especially hard-hit during the 1930s by the effects of overgrazing, persistent drought, and man-caused erosion. More recently, in the 1980s, the White Sands Missile Range was designated an alternative landing site for the U.S. Space Shuttle, should sites in south Florida and Southern California not be available.

Mesquite in early spring, Chihuahuan Desert, Texas

The plant most often associated with the Chihuahuan Desert is the lechuguilla agave. Each year, or at least in each year of good rain, an immense stalk rises from the thick, ground cluster of rigid, spiked green leaves. Once fully erect, this eight-to-ten-foot stalk produces an array of bright yellow flowers that are striking in their beauty, especially in contrast to the deep blue sky. In places, the plentiful agaves form miniature "woodlands" that are the bane of horsemen and cattlemen — the leaves are tipped with barbs as sharp as any instrument on a surgeon's tray. Creosote is another common plant of the Chihuahuan Desert, especially on arid flats where little else can grow. Up higher, on the mesas and in the limestone hills, you will notice that the Chihuahuan Desert experiences its primary wildflower season in the summer, as opposed to early spring, as is the case with the Mojave and Sonoran. Also, cactuses are not as common in the Chihuahuan Desert as elsewhere in the southwest. The only cactus of widespread interest in the Chihuahuan Desert is the peyote, a low, gray spineless plant that, when dried and consumed, produces visual hallucinations. Historically, the peyote was used by Indians in visionary religious rituals. Today, a permit from the federal government is required to possess the potent peyote "buttons." Eradication efforts on private and public lands have made the plant scarce north of the Rio Grande.

Ocotillo blossom, Chihuahuan Desert, Texas

Agave is the plant most often associated with the Chihuahuan Desert

Upland cactus, yucca, and cholla vegetation, Chihuahuan Desert, Texas

The animal that perhaps most symbolizes the Chihuahuan Desert is the coyote, a resourceful predator that can live on anything from kangaroo rats to acorns to mule deer. Coyotes gather in the late winter and early spring for mating. At that time the parents bond, excavate a natal den site, and subsequently remain together for the raising of the young. Their high-pitched yipping and howling evoke all that is wild and free in the desert wilderness. Another widespread animal of the Chihuahuan region is the gray mourning dove, whose soft, melancholy cooing can be heard around mesquite patches and desert springs. Despite being hunted widely, the dove is a prolific breeder and maintains its numbers throughout the area. The same is true of the coyote. One of the most distinctive animals of the Chihuahuan Desert is the Mexican free-tailed bat. These flying, insect-feeding mammals form immense colonies in caves and caverns. Perhaps the best known of these are found at the world-famous Carlsbad Caverns National Park in southern New Mexico.

The Chihuahuan Desert has moved from the stone age to the space age in just a few hectic generations. In some cases, the wildlife and landscape are still recovering from the effects of this rapid change. The desert is ancient and vast, though, and has a strength and resilience born of that physical maturity. It has witnessed the rise and fall of many animal nations. Our fate is of little concern in a landscape in which time is measured in geological ages. Dramas here — the erosion of a river canyon, the uplifting of a mountain range — take epochs to unfold. A million years of travail is represented by a line of crumbling fossils hidden behind a pricky pear cactus. Like any desert, the Chihuahuan has much to teach us about nature and life, especially the good life. It is a place to get outside of time for awhile, to listen to the

The green bark of the widespread paloverde tree is capable of photosynthesis. Chihuahuan Desert, Texas

song of oriole and the breeze in cottonwood leaves, to watch the sun rise and the sun set, to look up at the distant stars in renewed wonder.

DOWN BY THE RIVER: BIG BEND NATIONAL PARK

Half the pleasure of a visit to Big Bend National Park, as in certain other affairs, lies in the advance upon the object of our desire.... Like a castled fortification of Wagnerian gods, the Chisos Mountains stand alone in the morning haze, isolated and formidable, unconnected with other mountains, remote from any major range ... an emerald isle in a red sea.

—Edward Abbey

It is fitting that one of the largest national parks east of the Rocky Mountains should be in Texas, the largest state in the Lower 48. Big Bend National Park protects over 700,000 acres of desert lowlands and highlands, all nestled in a wide, wandering bend of the mighty Rio Grande River. The park, which is the size of Rhode Island, is a favored destination of Texas college students at spring break time, so be certain to consider that factor when making plans, especially if they include staying in park campgrounds. Big Bend is also popular in the winter months with the snowbirds, primarily because of the mild climate (December temperatures can be pleasantly warm, with little if any precipitation). Still, the park is one of the least visited of the larger parks, with only 297,000 visitors recorded in 1992. Compared with Great Smoky Mountains National Park (10 million annually) or Rocky Mountain National Park (3 million annually), Big Bend has much to offer in

The Mexican wolf may soon be restored to White Sands National Monument.   Photo courtesy of U.S. Fish and Wildlife Service

The coachwhip snake is common in the Chihuahuan Desert.
Photo courtesy of National Park Service

The tarantula is actually a very shy insect, and one important to the desert environment.   Photo courtesy of National Park Service

terms of solitude. Visitors should also check on Big Bend Ranch State Natural Area, a quarter-of-a-million-acre tract owned by the state of Texas, and located about 30 miles west of the national park. Here, too, one may experience the empty desert quarters (sans ranches, mines, and roads) of bygone days.

All through the Big Bend country there is the feel of the old western frontier. The landforms resonate with numerous rich historical associations. Here, for example, was the Great Comanche War Trail. Each autumn for hundreds of years, Comanche warriors tracked south into northern Mexico, looking for horses and cattle. When you drive through Persimmon Gap in the park, near the location of the Visitor's Center, you are following the ancient Comanche war trail. Eventually this route was followed by military troops and both Mexican and American settlers. In fact, the history of Big

Bend country reflects a rich intermixing of three cultures — Indian, Mexican and Anglo. Anyone with further interest in this fascinating subject should read Professor Elton Miles' definitive book *Tales of the Big Bend* (Texas A & M University Press, 1976).

The Chisos Mountains, a spectacular self-contained massif, serve as a natural geographic anchor for Big Bend National Park. The centrally located mountains are a complicated geological wonderland of volcanic plugs, igneous crags, forested buttes, jagged outcrops, wild dry pastures and bone-dry streams. Old horse paths and game trails criss-cross the range liberally. On some of those trails you may see bear tracks — black bears have recently recolonized the area from Mexico. Here are such magical places as Smugglers Gap, Lost Mine Peak, Panther Spring, Wasp Spring, Laguna Meadow, Tortuga (turtle) Mountain, and Emory Peak, which at 7825 feet is the tallest mountain in the park. The panoramic view from the south rim of the Chisos Mountains, looking out over thousands of square miles of desert wilderness in northern Mexico, is one of the finest in the national park system, comparable to the view of the Tetons from the Snake River overlook, the Grand Canyon from the North Rim, or Denali from the Moose Creek headwaters. To nature photographers, the place is an inspirational mecca to which each must journey at least once in a lifetime.

The other splendid part of the park is the Rio Grande River that forms the southern border of the park for 107 miles. Canyon walls here range from 1200 to 1600 feet (the height of a 120-story building!). Down along the river the thick subtropical vegetation forms a veritable jungle. Three great canyons are found along the Rio Grande in Big Bend — Santa Elena, Mariscal and Boquillas. Anyone curious about a Rio Grande rafting trip should read Edward Abbey's excellent essay "On The River Again" in his classic book *Abbey's Road*. Abbey writes eloquently of a "dreamlike river" in a "subterranean country of water and walls, with fluted gray limestone . . . tumbled boulders, banks of sand . . . clusters of bamboo twenty feet tall, thorny acacia in golden bloom spicing the air with a fragrance like that of apple blossoms." Its enough to make you want to drive down there right now!

As with the White Sands Missile Range in New Mexico, there has been some discussion in scientific and governmental circles as to restoring the Mexican wolf to the Big Bend country. The Mexican wolf is one of the most critically endangered mammals in the world, with virtually all remaining survivors in captivity. Only the California condor and the Florida panther are more threatened with extinction at the current time. For now, Big Bend National Park has been designated a natural recolonization area with the hope being that whatever wolves remain in Mexico (estimates range from 0 to 50 in the entire republic) will somehow find their way north to the Big Bend country. If they do, they will certainly find both habitat and prey (over 1,000 mule deer inhabit the park, as well as Sierra del Carmen white-tailed deer, jackrabbits, cottontails, and javelina). What's more, because the land is a designated national park, there are no hunting or trapping conflicts.

The problem with actively restoring wolves (as was the case with the Yellowstone wolves) is that local ranchers are concerned about depredations. Approximately 58,000 head of cattle, including 24,000 calves, are grazed annually in surrounding Brewster County, Texas. Any plan to restore the wolves will have to address these concerns. Until then, the captive wolves (currently over 100), are being kept in 19 enclosures scattered throughout the United States, where they are supervised by government biologists. Anyone who has ever seen a wolf in captivity has understood that wolves, like big cats, don't belong behind bars. They are forever pacing restlessly about their cages, their long legs yearning for the chase, their spirited eyes searching for the freedom of open horizons.

GETTING THERE

Big Bend National Park:
Access to the park is provided by three paved roads: U.S. 385 from Marathon, Texas to the North Entrance; State 118 from Alpine, Texas to the West Entrance, and Presidio to Study Butte on Ranch Road 170, then State 118 to the West Entrance. To reach Big Bend from El Paso, the closest city, drive east on Interstate 10 about 120 miles to Van Horn. Turn south on U.S. 90 to Alpine (108 miles), then turn south on State 118. Eighty miles later you'll pass through the town of Study Butte and enter the park on its western side. That's over 300 miles from El Paso!

Three other rare predators have lived in Big Bend in the past, and possibly still survive. First is the ocelot, a medium-sized spotted cat that preys on such animals as jackrabbits and javelina. There were two sightings in the period from 1980 through 1995, but nothing confirmed. Second is the jagaurundi, another endangered Texas cat, which, like the ocelot, is more common to the country south of the border. Ten jaguarundi sightings were reported by park visitors in the period from 1987 through 1995. Last on the list is the jaguar, which historically ranged along the Rio Grande and west into the Chiricahua Mountains of southeastern Arizona. It is unlikely that any of these big cats still range in Texas, where they are nevertheless still listed as an endangered species. Sad but true. Imagine rafting down the Rio Grande and suddenly spotting a golden-eyed jaguar in the shadowy green bamboo. One thinks of the lines from the poet William Blake: "What immortal hand or eye, dare frame thy fearful symmetry?"

Hard to believe a century ago such incidents would have not been the subject of mere fantasy.

Once in the park, you will find developed campgrounds at Chisos Basin, Rio Grande Village, and Cottonwood. The Visitor's Center is located at Panther Junction near the base of the Chisos Mountains. There is a second Visitor's Center about 25 miles to the southwest along the Rio Grande River. A road in this area leads to the magnificent Boquillas Canyon overlook.

One of the best times to visit Big Bend National Park is the autumn. The summer temperatures have diminished, most people are back in school or at work in the city, and the park campgrounds and trails are often refreshingly uncrowded. Autumn in the mild, southern-desert mountains is more subtle, but no less moving, than elsewhere in North America. For one thing, wild berries abound, including the bright red berries of the bush honeysuckle, the dark red berries of the redberry juniper, and the scarlet fruit of the Texas madrone. In the Chisos Mountains, the colors can be surprisingly beautiful. The leaves of Graves oak show a striking red, while the leaves of the gray oak gradually turn a yellowish-brown. Maples range from orange to red, depending on local factors such as genetics, soil and exposure. Wild sumac becomes vivid scarlet, and the buckeyes assume an amber color. Down below, in the desert, look for rust-colored hackberry. Along the Rio Grande, the magnificent cottonwoods exchange their summer green for prospector's gold, while the tamarisk along the river fades to a less intense shade of yellow.

One thing is certain. No matter what season you visit Big Bend, you will return home forever changed. Emerson was right when he wrote that "There is a relation between the hours of our life and the centuries of time.... The hours should be instructed by the ages, and the ages explained by the hours." The ages should inform the hours, and Big Bend is just the place for that quiet instruction to occur.

 ## POINTS OF INTEREST

BOQUILLAS CANYON TRAIL — The trailhead is located near the Boquillas Canyon overlook a few miles east of Boquillas Crossing, on the Rio Grande. Several other excellent trails are located in this area. Consult rangers for details.

CHISOS MOUNTAINS — The seven mile trail to the South Rim, which begins near the ranger station at the end of the road, is an absolute must for anyone able to walk fourteen miles. Even at a grandfatherly two-mile-an-hour pace, the trip would only require seven to eight hours. Be sure to carry sufficient water. For the more ambitious, an extensive two- or three-day circuit can be made of Juniper Canyon and Blue Creek Canyon via the Dodsen trail. Consult rangers for details.

DOG CANYON — A day hike to Dog Canyon or Devil's Den can be an enjoyable experience, and one accessed easily by the Dog Canyon roadside exhibit area, located about 3 miles south of the Permission Gap Visitor Center. Although there are no well-defined trails to Dog Canyon or Devil's End, there are old roadways and arroyos. Creosote is common here, as are prickly pear cactus and mesquite, the beans of which were an important food source for the Indians. Consult rangers for details.

RIO GRANDE RIVER — The river is popular with river rafters, who normally put in at Lajitas, near the confluence with Comanche Creek and float two to four days through Santa Elena Canyon, Mariscal Canyon, and Boquillas Canyon. The Park Service currently lists (without implying endorsement) four outfitters: Far Flung Adventures (800-359-4138); Outback Expeditions (800-343-1640); Big Bend River Tours (800-545-4240); Texas River Expeditions (800-839-7238).

SANTA ELENA CANYON TRAIL — This beautiful canyon trail is reached via the turnoff on Highway 118 near Maverick Mountain. Ansel Adams took one of his finest photographs of the Big Bend Country from this location.

A WILDERNESS OF SAND:
WHITE SANDS NATIONAL MONUMENT

Of all the western states I love New Mexico the best.
—Edward Abbey

Imagine the whitest sand in the world. A sand the color of fresh-fallen snow. A sand as fine as that found on the distant palm-shaded beaches of French Polynesia. A sand that forms lovely dunes such as you saw in the memorable Peter O'Toole film *Lawrence of Arabia*. Now imagine an inland sea of this sand, an extensive dune field filling part of a great basin with alkali flats, lava flows and desert savannas. Add two fault-block mountain

Sheep grazing in Big Bend area prior to the national park being formed.

Photo courtesy of Hill Collection, U.S.G.S.

ranges (San Adres and Oscura) of limestone rising heavily on either side of the basin, a deep blue New Mexican sky, the brilliant southwestern sun, experimental rockets arcing overhead occasionally from a nearby government missile range, and you have White Sands National Monument, a unique and priceless component of our national park system.

About a quarter of a billion years ago, when New Mexico was not even close to its current latitude and longitude, there was a shallow sea. At the bottom of that sea, sand gathered. Seas sometimes disappear, and such was

the case here. Over time, the accumulated sand of the now-dead sea, composed of gypsum — calcium sulfate — and of very substantial depth, was
slowly pushed upward in a dome-like formation. This occurred in the
Jurassic Period about 70 million years ago. The dinosaurs came and went and
gravity and time tirelessly worked together on the dome, grinding it down so
that an immense basin was formed. The mountains that you see to the east
and west of White Sands are remnants of the once-formidable sides of that
dome. In the center of the basin, the artful winds continually played with the
eroded Cenozoic sand, creating the beautiful dune fields — the miniature
Sahara — we see today.

Venturing out on the dunes, you may be fortunate enough to spot some
of the native wildlife, especially at dawn and dusk. In keeping with Darwin's
theory of natural selection and adaptation, these animals have changed their
color (or rather *had* their color changed by genes programmed to perpetuate
their own survival) so as to adapt to their blanched landscape. In White Sands
there are diminuitive, earless lizards as pale as the ice in an undefrosted freezer,
kit foxes that appear to have been taken by the tail and dipped into a bucket
of industrial-strength bleach. In both cases, their natural camouflage helps
these predators successfully stalk their prey. White-on-white is hard to see,
even to a mouse with eyes as bright and black
as night. Another animal you may see is the
oryx, an antelope native to Africa. These
sharp-horned antelope so common in zoologi-
cal parks were introduced to the area by the
New Mexican Game Department, primarily
for the benefit of big-game hunters. The "wild"
oryx enjoyed life in the Land of Enchantment,
so much so that their wandering numbers
(over 1700 animals!) now pose a threat to the
indigenous fauna and flora of the monument.

An animal once present at White Sands
— the Mexican wolf — may soon be restored to this part of southern New Mexico.
Barring unforseen developments, captive
Mexican wolves will be released in the White
Sands Missile Range in 1996. The operation
will proceed in a fashion similar to that
undertaken in Yellowstone in 1995. Initially,
large enclosures and local food sources will
be used (mule deer, pronghorn, small mam-

GETTING THERE

White Sands is the most
accessible park in the
Chihuahuan Desert. Driving
south from Albuquerque on
Interstate 25, exit at Las
Cruces (224 miles south)
and take U.S. 70 about 60
miles north to the monument
entrance, a few miles southwest of Alamogordo. The only
road access to White Sands
National Monument is pro-
vided by the Dunes Drive,
which begins on Highway
70/82 about 15 miles southwest of Alamagordo (or 54
miles northwest of Las
Cruces).

mals) to acclimate the wolves. After a period of months, the gates will be opened so that the wolves can come and go freely. Radio collars will enable scientists to follow closely the success of the reintroduction. Eventually, managers hope to have at least five family groups in the White Sands recovery area. The White Sands Missile Range is an ideal location for such a transplant, with its immense size and restricted public access as a missile impact zone.

To the west, the goal is to establish at least 15 family groups in the Blue Range area of east-central Arizona. Once approximately 120 wild wolves are distributed over 6,000 square miles of Arizona and New Mexico, the Mexican wolf — again, one of the world's most critically endangered mammals — will no longer be considered a threatened or endangered animal. The recovery plan calls for this delisting to occur as soon as the year 2004. Now that the red wolf has been restored to North Carolina (Alligator River National Wildlife Refuge, Great Smoky Mountains National Park) and the gray wolf to Idaho and Wyoming, it seems only logical and appropriate that the Mexican wolf be returned to its former haunts in the Southwest. In doing so we are making whole what past generations — in a different time, with different values —rendered incomplete.

Geronimo was active in the Chihuahuan Desert for years.

Photo courtesy of Western History Department, Denver Public Library

Dunes Drive leads eight miles into the heart of the monument. Exhibits along the way feature interesting aspects of the park's natural history. Various pullouts enable visitors to park and head off into dune fields of lovely parabola-like formations and extensive parallel ridges. For the less intrepid, there is a one-mile, self-guided nature trail. Unfortunately, there is no campground in the park, but there are three public

campgrounds within a half-hour drive of the park visitor center on
Highway 70/82.

White Sands is many things — the world's largest gypsum dune field, a
natural laboratory for studying genetic adaptations to the environment, a
photographer's paradise (Ansel Adams did some superb work here), an
immensely popular recreational area (over 600,000 visitors annually), a
good destination for a warm sunny walk on a short winter day, a sneak pre-
view of what twenty-first century astronauts may one day see on Mars.
There is literally no other place in the world quite like White Sands. A trip
to the dunes should be included on the itinerary of anyone travelling
through the Southwest.

OTHER SITES

ALAMEDA PARK ZOO — Located in downtown Alamogordo on U.S. 54,
the zoo includes animals of the desert (505-437-8430).

BOSQUE DEL APACHE NATIONAL WIDLIFE REFUGE — Designated in
1939 as a refuge and breeding ground for migratory birds, Bosque del Apache
now hosts over 100,000 migratory birds each winter, including 14,000 sand-
hill cranes, 50,000 snow geese, and 60,000 ducks. Various Chihuahuan
Desert amphibians, reptiles and mammals are also found in the refuge and its
environs. A 15-mile, one-way loop tour takes visitors deep into the refuge.
Bosque del Apache is located 20 miles south of Socorro, New Mexico on I-25
(San Antonio exit). For more information call 505-835-0424.

CARLSBAD CAVERNS NATIONAL PARK — The enormous caverns are
found in the foothills of the Gaudalupe Mountains about twenty miles
southwest of Carlsbad, New Mexico on U.S. 62/180. From late spring
through early fall, hundreds of thousands of bats fly out every evening from
the large upper chamber. The largest of the caverns measures 1800 feet in
length with a ceiling of 250 feet. Above ground, you will find classic
Chihuahuan Desert vegetation such as Texas sotol, lechuguilla agave, prickly
pear cactus, and octotillo, as well as walnut trees and gray oaks in the
canyons. Carlsbad is truly one of the wonders of the Chihuahuan Desert.

GUADALUPE MOUNTAINS NATIONAL PARK — Established in 1972, this
national park protects the four highest points in Texas (highest is 8,751 feet).
These starkly beautiful mountains are the remains of an immense, ancient

coral reef, with most of the reef now buried under the Texas plains. The park is relatively small — less than 100,000 acres — but has over 50 miles of hiking trails. In the high country there is a montane forest of Douglas fir and ponderosa pine, as well as a small herd of restored elk, mule deer, black bear, mountain lions and bighorn sheep. The lower canyons include vegetation more typical of the Chihuahuan Desert — Torrey yucca, prickly pear cactus, Texas madrona, creosote, sotol, and lechuguilla agave. The nearest major city is El Paso, Texas, located about 110 miles to the southwest. Carlsbad is 55 miles to the northeast.

LIVING DESERT STATE PARK — This unusual state park about four miles northwest of Carlsbad, New Mexico on U.S. 285 has over 50 species of desert animals in their natural habitats, as well as a greenhouse of cactuses, a prairie dog village, and an interesting visitor center (505-887-5516).

FURTHER INFORMATION

Big Bend National Park
Texas 79834
915-477-2236

Guadalupe Mountains National Park
3225 National Parks Highway
Carlsbad, New Mexico 88220

Carlsbad Caverns National Park
3225 National Parks Highway
Carlsbad, New Mexico 88220
505-785-2232

White Sands National Monument
PO Box 458
Alamogordo, New Mexico 88310
505-479-6124

V

The Great Basin Desert

Visibly our new home was a desert, walled in by barren, snow-clad mountains. There was not a tree in sight. There was no vegetation but the endless sagebrush and greasewood. All nature was gray with it. We were plowing through great deeps of powdery alkali dust that rose in thick clouds and floated across the plain like smoke from a burning house. We were coated with it like millers; so were the coach, the mules, the mailbags, the driver — we and the sagebrush and the other scenery were one monotonous color. Long trains of freight wagons in the distance enveloped in ascending masses of dust suggested pictures of prairies on fire. These teams and their masters were the only life we saw. Otherwise we moved in the midst of solitude, silence, and desolation. Every twenty steps we passed the skeleton of some dead beast of burden, with its dust-coated skin stretched tightly over its empty ribs. Frequently a solemn raven sat upon the skull or the hips and contemplated the passing coach with meditative serenity.

—Mark Twain
Roughing It

THE GREAT BASIN is the largest desert in the continental United States. It covers virtually all of northern and central Nevada, as well as portions of western Utah, southern Oregon and Idaho, southwestern Wyoming and northwestern Colorado. This expansive region between the Sierra Nevadas and the Rocky Mountains is known by geographers as the "basin and range" country, and is home to over 150 separate mountain ranges and associated basins. The Great Basin is, like parts of the Mojave, a high altitude desert, with valleys sinking as low as 4000 feet and alpine peaks reaching past 12,000 feet. As recently as 10,000 years ago, many of these enormous valleys were filled with water. Geologists believe that Lake Bonneville, the largest Pleistocene

Impact crater from nuclear detonation, Great Basin Desert (Nevada)

lake of the Great Basin, was more than half the size of Ohio and covered parts of Utah, Nevada, and Idaho. In places, the lake was more than 1,000 feet deep! Now-extinct species such as mammoths, camels, Asiatic horses, cave bears, ground sloths, and stag-moose lived and died along its shores, and millions of waterfowl fished and flew among the shallows. As the climate of the northern hemisphere warmed at the end of the Ice Age, the giant lakes of the Great Basin evaporated and became sandy deserts and salt basins. Today, for example, only the Great Salt Lake and the Bonneville Salt Flats remain as living testaments of the once colossal natural resevoir known as Lake Bonneville.

Unlike the other American deserts, the Great Basin is a "cold" desert, receiving most of its precipitation in the form of winter snow. Temperatures as low as minus 20 degrees Fahrenheit have been recorded. As a result, the physical appearance of the Great Basin is dramatically different from that of the other deserts. For one thing, there are fewer of the succulent plants so often associated with North American deserts — the conspicuous barrel and large flat-padded cactuses, the familiar agaves, the sharp-spined yucca. For

Wild horse, Great Basin Desert (Utah)

another, the classic trees of the desert creeks down south — most notably the paloverde and willow — are absent.

The first Euro-american explorers of the Great Basin were the Spanish fathers, Dominguez and Escalante, who entered the region from the south in 1776, the same year Jefferson was writing the Declaration of Independence back in Philadelphia. They wandered widely, never quite certain where they were, and frequently becoming lost, but they always succeeded in at least trying to convert the native residents. Within a few decades, what became known as "The Old Spanish Trail" ran from the vicinity of present-day Salt Lake City to Los Angeles, touching on portions of the Great Basin and Painted deserts along the way. The first American to cross the Great Basin Desert was Jedediah Smith. From 1826 through 1829, the legendary frontiersman explored east from the Yosemite region in California to the Wasatch Range in Utah, and then south to Needles on the Colorado River.

Not long after, the expedition of French-born Benjamin Bonneville (1832–1834), ranging west from the South Pass on the Oregon Trail, explored the region from the Great Salt Lake to the Sierra Nevadas. The first truly scientific survey of the Great Basin was that of John Fremont in 1845, who studied the area from the Great Salt Lake west to the Humboldt River in what is today Nevada. Later Clarence King, whose reports read as well as anything by Muir or Burroughs, conducted important surveys of the region, as did George Wheeler. With the completion of the Pacific Railroad Survey (1853–1854) and the construction of the first transcontinental railroad (Council Bluffs, Iowa to San Francisco, California), the Great Basin was opened to settlement.

In the years that followed, western migration more or less bypassed the Great Basin, seeking the rich "Arcady" that was and is the Pacific coast of California. The Great Basin became a place to drive through quickly, or fly over. Many years of relative obscurity passed. Then, in 1950, the Great Basin was abruptly thrust into the international spotlight as President Harry Truman designated the Nevada Test Site for nuclear testing. The vast military reservation is located north of Mercury, Nevada and spreads over the transition zone between the Great Basin Desert and the Mojave Desert. It was selected because operations were difficult and expensive in the South Pacific, and there were concerns — this was during the Cold War — that a Soviet commando operation might be mounted to permanently borrow some technology, technicians, and/or bombs. The desert seemed like the perfect place — remote, desolate and vitually uninhabited — to safely perfect weapons of mass destruction.

Six weeks after the site was established, five bombs were tested. These powerful devices were dropped by air force bombers and detonated at various altitudes over the floor of the desert. The explosions rocked the fledgling boomtown of Las Vegas with the power of major earthquakes, breaking windows, moving heavy furniture around and scattering household items. Eventually there were hundreds of nuclear tests at the Nevada site. In many cases radiation spread downwind to cities like St. George, Utah, which to this day records elevated cancer deaths from years of radiation exposure. Probably as a result of this experience with nuclear programs, local residents rose up in protest during the 1980s against the proposed mobile missile defense system — forming the Great Basin MX Alliance — and successfully defeated the plan.

Ironically, many of the secret government and military sites in the Great

Rabbit brush, Great Basin Desert (Nevada)

Basin Desert are now valued by
ecologists as wildlife refuges. Here,
for decades, species were protected
from livestock grazing, open-pit
mining, and unbridled development (Reno and Las Vegas). These
include such rare and/or endangered species as the desert tortoise,
kit fox, kangaroo mouse, spotted
bat, Lahontan cutthroat trout, Gila
monster, prairie falcon, goshawk,
Nevada primrose, and various milk
vetch, to name just a few.

By far, the most characteristic
plant of the Great Basin Desert is
the big-leafed sage. It is everywhere,
from ravines to ridgetops, from
bushy riverbanks to the most barren alkali flats. Mark Twain, who
lived and worked in Nevada during
his youth, described the sage as:

Mule deer skeleton, Great Basin Desert (Nevada)

> *. . . a gnarled and venerable live oak tree reduced to a little shrub
> two feet high . . . [It] is a grayish green, and gives that tint to
> desert and mountain. It smells like our domestic sage . . . and is
> a singularly hardy plant [growing] among barren rocks, where
> nothing else in the vegetable world would grow . . . Sagebrush is
> very fair fuel [for a campfire], but as a vegetable it is a distin-
> guished failure. Nothing can abide the taste of it but the jackass
> and his illegitimate child the mule. But their testimony to its
> nutritiousness is worth nothing, for they will eat . . . anthractic
> coal, or old bottles, and then go off looking as grateful as if they
> had had oysters for dinner.*

All around the fringes of the Great Basin, with increased annual rainfall,
the native grasses become more noticeable, and gradually a more steppe-like
vegetation replaces the desert. But through the vast heart of the desert the
humble sagebrush reigns supreme.

The two animals most associated with the Great Basin are the feral horse, some of which are descended from those that escaped Cortez and Coronado in the sixteenth century, and the coyote, which has maintained a continued presence in the region since the Ice Age, despite the best efforts of government trappers and local woolgrowers. Of the coyote, Mark Twain wrote humorously:

> *The coyote is a living, breathing allegory of Want. He is always hungry. He is always poor, out of luck, and friendless. The meanest creatures despise him, and even the fleas would desert him ... He does not mind going a hundred miles to breakfast, and a hundred and fifty to dinner, because he is sure to have three or four days between meals, and he can just as well be traveling and looking at the scenery as lying around doing nothing.*

Visitors can also expect to see their share of pronghorn antelope, which normally will begin running as soon as the car is stopped (suggesting a previous acquaintance with poachers).

   One of the country's most critically endangered mammals, the black-footed ferret, was historically found in the eastern parts of the Great Basin Desert. This range included southwestern Wyoming, western Colorado and eastern Utah. The problem with the ferret, as was noted earlier, is that it is

Big leaf sage, Vermillion Cliffs Wilderness Area, Great Basin Desert

Riparian bottomland, Great Basin Desert

almost entirely dependent on one food resource: prairie dogs. As stockmen (operating on public lands) poisoned one prairie dog colony after another, the ferrets similarly disappeared. So effective were the eradication efforts that today the prairie dog is listed as an endangered species in the state of Utah. At this writing the ferret exists only in a breeding colony and at several other areas where they are being experimentally returned to the wild. One of these sites is located in southwestern Wyoming on the fringes of the Great Basin Desert. With a little help from its (human) friends, the ferret may just be pulled back from the brink of extinction, and once again inhabit the desert, steppe and grassland habitats of the West.

The Great Basin offers a welcome respite from the neon casinos, singing lounge lizards, and gaudy floorshows of the desert boomtowns. Here, just a few miles from crime-filled cities and crowded interstate highways, the traveler can enter an older and richer world, a place of serenity and silence, beauty and truth. Valleys roll away forever. Snow-topped peaks dot the horizon. Sage sparrows sing. Honeybees drain wildflowers. And always, from somewhere far away, a dry wind blows, carrying with it the recent memory of sage and the promise of another magnificent vista just over that distant hill. Here is the age-old demesne of the mountain lion and the mule deer, the rattlesnake and the rabbit. Here is the quiet splendor of our most under-loved desert, the Great Basin.

WILD HORSES AND WILY COYOTES: BLM AND NATIONAL WILDLIFE REFUGE LANDS IN NEVADA, OREGON, COLORADO AND UTAH

BLACK ROCK DESERT ROADLESS AREA

It was a country which had nothing of a redeeming character.
It seemed to be the River of Death dried up...It was enlivened
by the murmur of no streams, but was a wide desolation.
—Anonymous 1846 diarist on the
California Trail

There are multitudes of BLM natural areas, wilderness areas, or wilderness study areas in the Great Basin Desert. Our focus here will be on a handful of the more representative. One of the best in this respect is the 640,000 acre Black Rock Wilderness Study Area in northwestern Nevada. The nearest town of note is Winnemucca. The roadless area encompasses the fossilized lake bed of Lake Lahontan, an Ice Age reservoir that once filled the region. At the bottom of the basin, you will find the sagebrush and greasewood so characteristic of the Great Basin Desert. The highest peak of note (Pahute) reaches to 8,494 feet. The area is well known for its widespread Pleistocene fossils, rich archaeological sites, and tremendous beauty. There are salt playas and alkaline lakes at lower elevations, with distant juniper-and-pinyon-covered mountains that appear like floating clouds on hot days.

Black Rock thermal springs run at temperatures above 130 degrees Fahrenheit — be forewarned. There is a story that in pioneer days a team of dehydrated oxen bolted from their wagons and fell into the springs, where they were boiled to death. It is a country rich in myth, legend, and folklore; the traditional homeland of the Paiute, Bannock and Shoshone; the former domain of prospectors; the last dusty desert for California homesteaders; the stomping grounds of cattlemen and woolgrowers. In short, a perfect place to go these days, if the high desert and plenty of solitude is your definition of paradise.

GETTING THERE

Black Rock Wilderness Study Area: Driving north on U.S. 95 from Winnemucca, Nevada, access is via undeveloped roads from Highways 140 and I-80.

Magenta prickly pear cactus blossom, Great Basin Desert (Nevada)

GREAT SALT LAKE DESERT

After supper, we would spread out our sleeping bags in a circle,
heads pointing to the center like a covey of quail, and watch the
Great Basin sky fill with stars. Our attachment to the land was our
attachment to each other.

> —Terry Tempest Williams,
> *Refuge: An Unnatural History*
> *of Family and Place*

The Great Salt Lake — all that remains of the much larger prehistoric
Lake Bonneville — is a central feature of the Great Basin Desert in Utah. To
the west of the Salt Lake are two enormous
BLM roadless areas, North Great Salt Lake
Desert (850,000 acres) and South Great Salt
Lake Desert (1,144,000 acres). This desert
country is geographically more like the coun-
try over the border in Nevada than the rest of
Utah. Lowlands descend to salt flats. In peri-
ods of heavy rainfall, however, these fossil
lakes refill and threaten to flood the interstate.
Pine-speckled mountains rise dramatically

GETTING THERE

Great Salt Lake Desert is
basically everything south
and north of Interstate 80 in
western Utah from exit 62 to
the Nevada State Line.

here and there, sometimes topped with bristlecone pines. For many people, driving west from Salt Lake City on Interstate 80, this is their first real taste of the Great Basin Desert, and it is a formidable taste. The area is so bleak and empty that the sage steppe and snow-capped peaks of Nevada seem lush by comparison. There is a scenic viewpoint just over the border in Nevada near the exit for U.S. 93, which leads south to Great Basin National Park.

HART MOUNTAIN NATIONAL ANTELOPE RANGE AND CHARLES SHELDON NATIONAL ANTELOPE REFUGE

> Sooner or later the West must accept the limitations imposed by aridity, one of the chief of which is a restricted human population … the boosters have been there from the beginning to oversell the West as Garden of the World, the flowing well of opportunity, the stomping ground of the self-reliant.
> — Wallace Stegner, Introduction to *Where the Bluebird Sings to the Lemonade Springs*

These two refuges, located in southern Oregon and northwestern Nevada respectively, were established in the 1930s to protect the habitat of the prong-

Blue penstemon blossoming from rock wall, Great Basin Desert (Utah)

GETTING THERE

To reach **Hart Mountain**
drive north from Lakeview on
U.S. 395 for 5 miles. Turn
east on State Route 140 for
28 miles and turn north on
the undeveloped road to
Plush. Follow this for about
41 miles to the refuge. To
reach the **Charles Seldon
Refuge** follow State Route
140 east of Lakeview, Oregon
for about 55 miles to the
Nevada state line.

horn, that elusive fleetfooted essence of the
Great Basin Desert. The Oregon refuge preserves pronghorn breeding areas. The Sheldon
Refuge in Nevada was created to save their
winter range from development. Together, the
two refuges protect over 800,000 acres, an
area twice the size of Rocky Mountain
National Park. Hart Mountain is anchored by
a spectacular 8,065-foot fault-block ridge that
is broken cliff on one side and rolling sage
country on the other. The Sheldon Refuge, by
contrast, is characterized by rolling hills and
wide open valleys, basaltic mesas and wandering canyons. Charles Sheldon, by the way, was
a pioneering conservationist responsible for
the establishment of Mount McKinley
National Park (1917) in Alaska. An interesting
historical subject, he graduated from Yale, made a fortune in a Mexican mining venture, and then retired to a life of big-game hunting, book writing and
fighting for various preservation causes.

The refuges are accessed via U.S. 395 in northern Nevada, and Oregon
140 in southern Oregon.

SMOKE CREEK DESERT ROADLESS AREA

GETTING THERE

**Smoke Creek Desert
Roadless Area:** Access is via
Nevada State 447, on BLM
roads west of Gerlach and
Empire, Nevada. Take
Interstate 80 east of Reno to
Exit 46. Turn north on State
Route 447 and continue on
to Empire and Gerlach, about
50 miles to the north.

You may walk the deserts of the Great
Basin the bloom time of the year, all
the way across from the snowy Sierra
to the snowy Wasatch, and your eyes
will be filled with many a gay malva,
and poppy, and abronia, and cactus.
        —John Muir, *Steep Trails*

The Smoke Creek Desert Roadless Area
(148,000 acres) is one of the best locations in
the Great Basin Desert to view wild horses.
The BLM management area is located north
of the Pyramid Lake Indian Reservation and
south of the Granite Range along the

California border. This is less than a two-hour drive from Reno, a popular tourist attraction. What you will find in the Smoke Creek Desert are not slot machines and floor shows, but prickly pear and sagebrush, grouse and golden eagles, pronghorn and mule deer. The mustangs are the largest mammals on the range, and are easily spotted at a distance. They travel in harem groups ruled by a stallion. There will be mares both old and young, colts and yearlings, and if you get too close they will gallop off, their manes flying, their hoofs pounding, and leaving a trail of dust suspended in the air. There are few sights more stirring to see in the West — evoking as they do so many deep cultural memories of the frontier — than wild horses at full gallop over open, unfenced ground.

VERMILLION CREEK ROADLESS AREA

To the east we look up the valley of the Vermillion, through which Fremont found his way to the great parks of Colorado.
—John Wesley Powell,
Journals

Located in extreme northwestern Colorado, the Vermillion Creek Roadless Area is one of the least known and most beautiful natural areas in the state. Although Colorado is famous for its overcrowded national parks and forests, here is a place where you can enjoy nature — and the easternmost portion of the Great Basin Desert — in peace and quiet. Only during the fall hunting season (pronghorn and mule deer) will you encounter other people in the area. Vermillion Creek (88,340 acres) includes badlands reminiscent of those in Anza-Borrego State Park (Southern California), rolling sage flats identical to those that cover the state of Nevada, deeply eroded rock canyons, petroglyphs, ancient seabed fossil formations, and, as the name, indicates, beautiful scarlet cliffs and rock outcroppings.

Hikes could include a walk up Vermillion Creek or an approach from the east through a

GETTING THERE

The **Vermillion Basin** is located about 80 miles west of Craig, Colorado, via U.S. 40 and State Route 318, or due south from Rock Springs, Wyoming on a good paved road that becomes a decent gravel road (Moffat County Road 10N) at the state line. Drive west of the little town of Maybell on State Route 318 for 39 miles to the junction with State Route 430. Drive north on this undeveloped road into the Vermillion Creek uplands.

Black widow spider, Great Basin Desert
Photo courtesy of U.S. Fish and Wildlife Service

gap in the Vermillion Bluffs. The colors in this area are spectacular.

Vermillion Creek Roadless Area is at the margins of the Great Basin Desert and the shortgrass prairie, with a little bit of the Rocky Mountains thrown in for effect. You will see classic Great Basin vegetation here — big-leafed sage, prickly pear cactus, pinyon pine, juniper — but you also may see a misplaced Douglas fir or run into an errant band of wapiti, both more common to the big mountains rising to the east. The fact that it has not been recommended for wilderness status by the BLM has probably saved it. There are numerous other BLM roadless areas in the region that will also be blank spots on the map for the next century or so.

BRISTLECONES ON ICE:
GREAT BASIN NATIONAL PARK

In a little while quite a number of peaks swung into view with long claws of glittering snow clasping them; and with here and there, in the shade, down the mountainside, a little solitary patch of snow looking no larger than a lady's pocket handkerchief, but being in reality as large as a 'public square.'

—Mark Twain, *Roughing It*

This new (1986) national park, the only national park in Nevada, protects a representative mountain range in the region. An important part of the Great Basin Desert are the numerous fault-block mountains — over 100 — that sharply wrinkle the otherwise flattened landscape. Although the surrounding lowlands receive only about 10 inches of annual precipitation, the Snake Range receives up to 35 inches a year, resulting in grassy meadows, thick forests, and lingering snowfields. The area is famous for its bristlecone pine, some of which are known, through core-boring, to be over 4,000 years old. The oldest recorded bristlecone in the park was 4,950 years old. Think about that for a moment. Nearly five thousand years ago. At that time Sargon of Akkad was not born yet, nor Hammurabai, nor any of the other influential figures at the dawn of western history. They were all hundreds of years in the future, after the birth of civilization in that other desert along the Euphrates. Touch one of these ancient trees and you are touching something older than time, as measured by the human word. Amazing — another one of the marvels hidden in the Great Basin region.

The Snake Range protected by the park includes 13 peaks over 11,000 feet, as well as the soaring granitic spires of Wheeler Peak (13,063 feet). The Wheeler Peak Scenic Drive provides visitors to Great Basin with superb views of the Snake Range, as it climbs over 3,000 feet in 12 miles, from semi-desert woodlands of pinyon and juniper to forests of spruce and fir identical to those found in the far north of Canada. At the end of the road there is a trail to the top of Wheeler Peak. Down below, in the vicinity of the turn-off for Wheeler Peak Drive, you will find one of the important features of the park — Lehman Caves. These extensive caverns are really something to see, with fantastic displays of stalagtites, stalagmites, sculpted stone columns, rock curtains, and mushroom-like formations. A tour of the cave is highly recommended. Emerging from the cave into blinding Great Basin sun, you feel like one of the inhabitants of Plato's Cave coming back to the world. Such a subterranean experience always changes your perspective on the planet's surface.

In Great Basin National Park we encounter a high, mountain landscape that was shaped by glaciers, and not by rain and wind as on the lower desert. It is a spectacular range, and I am grateful for the park, but it

GETTING THERE

Great Basin National Park is located east of Ely, Nevada near the Utah state line. Follow U.S. 50 for 57 miles east of Ely to the junction of State 487. Turn south on State Route 487 for 5 miles to Baker, Nevada, then turn west on State Route 488. The Visitor Center is located 6 miles down the road.

would say something wonderful about us as a people — our values, our insights, our aesthetics — if we were to designate a second Great Basin National Park on the desert floor, which is no less beautiful in its own austere way than the mountains of the region. Given the fact that most of Nevada is BLM or National Forest land, finding and designating such a location would seem not to be a geographic problem, only a political one.

JURASSIC PARK:
DINOSAUR NATIONAL MONUMENT

When we return to camp at noon the sun shines in splendor on vermillion walls, shaded into green and gray where the rocks are lichened over; the river fills the channel from wall to wall, and the canyon opens, like a beautiful portal, to a region of glory.
—John Wesley Powell,
Journals

The Gates of Lodore, Echo Park, Split Mountain Canyon, all evoke the epic adventure of John Wesley Powell, who floated the Green River in 1869 despite the assertions of trappers, Indians, and others who said it could not be done. Powell, with quintessential frontier daring, proved them all wrong, and in the process discovered a country remarkable not only for its red sandstone cliffs, bottomless gorges, dramatically uplifted plateaus, and other exotic landforms, but also for its rich treasure-trove of dinosaur bones. The first person to excavate the area was Earl Douglas, from the Carnegie Museum of Pittsburgh, who in 1909 located an enormous quantity of bones in what appears to have been a mass death site for dinosaurs. Six years later the quarry, and its surroundings, were set aside for management by the Park Service. In 1938 the monument was greatly expanded. During the 1950s, plans surfaced to dam Echo Park, but legions of outraged defenders rose up in protest to defeat the ill-begotten proposal. Unfortunately, they were not so lucky at Glen Canyon farther to the south.

GETTING THERE

Dinosaur National Monument: From Interstate 70 exit 15 west of Grand Junction, drive north on State Route 139 to Rangeley, and turn west on State Route 64. Nineteen miles further on turn east on U.S. 40 for two miles until you reach the access road to the monument. The Visitor's Center, and the Echo Park Campground, are at the end of this 18-mile road.

Crossing the Great Basin Desert in Utah, 40th Parallel Expedition (King Survey).
Photo courtesy of U.S.G.S.

There are many good hiking trails in Dinosaur (224,156 acres), which provide a mixture of Painted Desert geographic features and Great Basin Desert fauna and flora. The Ruple Point Trail (4 miles one way) leads through sagebrush desert flats and woodlands of pinyon pine and juniper to a panoramic viewpoint above Island Park and the mouth of Split Mountain Canyon. Similarly, the Jones Hole Trail (also 4 miles one way) provides a nice walk in the desert, albeit along the banks of a stream. At the end of the trail you will be on the banks of the Green River. Many visitors to the monument float down the Green River or the Yampa River, and in the process see sheer, 1500-foot cliffs, Class V whitewater rapids, and other wonders of the canyon country.

FURTHER INFORMATION

Bureau of Land Management
Regional Headquarters
Office of Public Affairs
Denver Federal Center
Lakewood, Colorado 80215
303-239-3600

Dinosaur National Monument
PO Box 210
Dinosaur, Colorado 81610
303-374-2468

Committee for Idaho's High Desert
PO Box 463
Boise, Idaho 83701

Great Basin National Park
Baker, Nevada 89311
702-234-7331

Great Basin Naturalist. This monograph was founded in 1939 and is published from one to four times a year. Issues are often devoted to the fauna and flora of the Great Basin. Subscriptions can be obtained from: The Editor, *Great Basin Naturalist,* 290 Life Science Museum, Brigham Young University, Provo, Utah 84602.

Friends of Nevada Wilderness
PO Box 8096
Reno, Nevada 89507
702-322-2867
BLM District Office
1280 Industrial Avenue
Craig, Colorado 81625
303-824-4441

Nevada Biodiversity Initiative
Department of Biology, 314
University of Nevada
Reno, NV 89557-0015
702-784-4565

Oregon Natural Resources Council
1050 Yeon Building
522 SW 5th Avenue
Portland, Oregon 97204
503-223-9001

Sheldon-Hart Mountain National
    Antelope Refuges
Box 111
Lakeview, Oregon 97630
The Wildlands Project
117 East Fifth Street, Suite F
PO Box 1276
McMinnville, Oregon 97128
503-434-9848

Toiyabe National Forest
1200 Franklin Way
Sparks, Nevada 89431
702-331-6444

Utah Wilderness Coalition
PO Box 11446
Salt Lake City, Utah 84147

VI

The Painted Desert

The canyon country of southern Utah and northern Arizona — the Colorado Plateau — is
something special. Something strange, mar-
velous, full of wonders. As far as I know there is
no other region on earth much like it, or even
remotely like it. Nowhere else have we had this
lucky combination of vast sedimentary rock formations exposed to a desert climate, a great
plateau carved by major rivers — the Green, the
San Juan, the Colorado — into such a surreal
land of form and color.
— Edward Abbey, "Come on In"
from *The Journey Home*

ABBEY WAS RIGHT. This unique desert province of North America is like
no other. Here are such marvels as the Grand Canyon, Glen Canyon, and
countless other named and unnamed canyons. The free-standing arches,
exotic rock cities, colorful reefs, gaping barrancas, and distant snow-capped
peaks make the Painted Desert, an eastern extension of the Great Basin
Desert, a realm unto itself. No one can say they've experienced all the natural
glory of the American deserts until they have seen the Painted Desert. Like
parts of the Mojave and most of the Great Basin, the Painted Desert is a high
desert, with altitudes frequently beginning at 5000 feet. Much of the annual
precipitation, which is in the neighborhood of ten inches, comes as snow.
Summers tend to be hot — though not as scalding as down south — and
winters are cool and sometimes cold (below zero). By far, what most distin-

Prehistoric rock drawings, Newspaper Rock State Park, Utah

guishes the Great Basin are the otherwordly geological structures — the great barrancas and associated side canyons that deeply incise the Colorado Plateau. It is in this region — over 150,000 square miles in size — that some of the most spectacular national parks in America can be found, making the Painted Desert a truly international treasure.

The Painted Desert was the traditional home of the Anasazi Indians, commonly known as the "cliff dwellers." These archaic peoples lived, and apparently flourished, in the region from approximately A.D. 850 to A.D. 1250. Their sturdy sandstone homes and rock-sheltered towns are visible at such places as Mesa Verde National Park and Hovenweep National Monument. Scientists believe that a period of prolonged drought forced the Anasazi to migrate out of the area, probably to more reliable river basins to the east, such as the Rio Grande. Hundreds of years later, as the climate became slightly less dry, new Athabaskan-speaking immigrants from the north — the Navajo and Apache — moved through and into the area. These tribes persist to this day, with the Navajo living on the largest Indian reservation in the contiguous United States. It is on the Navajo reservation that the famed Monument Valley is found, the majestic landscape that has been memorialized in such films as *Stagecoach* (1939) and *The Greatest Story Ever Told* (1965).

The first American to see the Painted Desert was Jedediah Smith, who crossed what is now Utah on his legendary walkabout of 1826–1829. Smith entered the country from the north, following the Wasatch Mountains south to the Seveier River and then to the Virgin River. The next to arrive was John C. Fremont of the U.S. Corps of Topographical Engineers, who in 1842 led an expedition in the opposite direction, entering the desert from the

Red sandstone in the backcountry of Canyonlands National Park, Utah

southwest and exiting through the Uintah Mountains. Neither Smith nor Fremont penetrated the desert lands very far and the interior of the region remained a tantalizing mystery. About ten years later, the Pacific Railroad Survey of Gunnison and Beckwith essentially ignored the Painted Desert, and it was not until the period after the Civil War, with the Powell survey, that the Painted Desert finally began to be mapped and studied.

Major John W. Powell, a one-armed Civil War veteran, personally led a team of nine geologists, cartographers, photographers, scouts and adventurers across what was then the Utah Territory. The Painted Desert was the last great *terra incognita* in the American West and Powell aimed to put it on the map. His account of the expedition, which included the first (and incredibly perilous) descent of the Colorado River through the Grand Canyon, is now considered one of the classics in exploration literature. In a passage selected almost at random from Powell's book, *The Exploration of the Colorado River*, one sees what a typical day on the expedition was like:

> *... the waters reel and roll and boil, and we are scarcely able to determine where we can go. Now the boat is carried to the right ... [now] she is shot into the stream ... and is dragged over to the other side, where, caught in a whirlpool, she spins about. We can neither land nor run as we please. The boats are entirely unmanageable; no order in their running can be preserved ... each crew [is] laboring for its own preservation. In such a place we come to another rapid. Two of the boats run it perforce. One succeeds in landing ... [the other] drifts unmanageable. Breaker after breaker rolls over her and one capsizes her. The men are thrown out; but they cling to the boat, and she drifts down some distance ... the oars are lost ... Then for two miles we find smooth water.*

The vegetation of the Painted Desert is much like that of its parent region, the Great Basin. You won't find the larger succulent and arboreal cactuses of the southern deserts here, but you will find the prickly pear, with its beautiful sulphur-colored flowers, and the claret cup cactus, with blossoms the color of wine. Sagebrush is common, as might be expected for a province of the Great Basin Desert, as is creosote and saltbush. In higher regions there are pinyon pines, whose nuts were so prized by the Anasazi. Scattered among the pinyons are the ubiquitous junipers, that were so cherished by Edward Abbey for their stark, indefatigable beauty.

The animal life of the desert is similar to that found in the Rocky

Chessler Park, Canyonlands National Park, Utah

Mountains and the Great Basin. Mule deer are widespread, from the ridgetops to the canyon bottoms, as are various rodent tribes — ground squirrels, chipmunks, woodrats, prairie dogs. And of course wherever you

A typical scene in the beautiful outback of the Painted Desert, Utah

Towering rock formations in Arches National Park, Utah

have rodents, you have their nemesis, the coyote. In riparian and upland areas you'll sometimes find the tracks of bobcats and mountain lions. The bird most associated with the Painted Desert is the golden eagle, often

Delicate arch with La Sal Mountains in background, Arches National Park, Utah

spotted soaring among the cumulus clouds. The sight of a golden eagle rising on the thermals over the Grand Canyon can cause even the most cyni-
cal city-dweller to stop and stare. Every fall, bird-watchers gather on the
rims of the Grand Canyon to watch as dozens, and sometimes hundreds, of
raptors — falcons, hawks, eagles — migrate south over the region
(although in recent years their numbers have dropped alarmingly). Another
very common bird, and one that figured prominently in the mythology of
Indians, is the raven. This is a surprisingly large bird, with a thick bill and
a shaggy ruff at the throat. Its distinctive cry is the very essence of Painted
Desert country. Reptiles are everywhere, especially the green collared lizard,
a kind of hyperactive canyon sprite; the bull snake (which feeds on
rattlesnakes); and the cute little horned lizard, which has an unlikely crown
of one-inch spikes and looks like a miniature version of a ten-ton dinosaur
(and probably is).

Federal biologists are currently studying three sites in the Painted Desert
of northern Arizona — Vermillion Cliffs and Echo Cliffs near Page and
Prospect Valley just south of Grand Canyon National Park — for the possible release of endangered California condors. The last confirmed sighting of
a condor in northern Arizona was in 1924 near Flagstaff. Researchers hope to
release captive-bred condors from cliff sites that will provide the sort of isolated habitat necessary for the big birds. Currently (1996) the Vermillion
Cliffs site is preferred, as it has an abundance of open public lands, nesting
escarpments, and plenty of food sources. Local ranchers seem willing to
accommodate the condors, and are primarily concerned with the effects
increased tourism might have on their operations. At this writing, the only
condors in the wild are flying around the Los Padres National Forest
(Sisquoc and Sespe Condor Sanctuaries) near Santa Barbara, California. The
major sources of mortality on the condors in the past were power lines,
poaching and illegally poisoned carcasses. With any luck, you may one day
be able to show your children a bird that survived the Ice Age, and then
almost became extinct in our own time.

The Colorado Plateau region, and its associated environs, is a wonderland. It is a place that has always reminded me of the world's largest outdoor
church (or synagogue, or temple). A place fit for prayer and reflection. With
amphitheaters built to hold one million comfortably. And daily celestial displays of thunder, lightning, snow, rain, stars, and meteors. All in such a way
as to bring us closer to whatever it is that made, and continues to make, this
green, singing world. *Grateful.* That is the word that articulates how I feel
about the Canyon Country. Grateful that we have it here in America, and
don't have to fly to the Gobi to see it. Grateful that it is there when I am lost

and need to be found, broken and need to be fixed, out of tune and need to be brought back into harmony. Grateful that it will be there for my son and his son, until finally there are no sons, only the world and the sun.

ABBEY COUNTRY:
ARCHES NATIONAL PARK AND
CANYONLANDS NATIONAL PARK

This is the most beautiful place on earth.
—Edward Abbey

No one can visit Arches or Canyonlands country without first reading Edward Abbey's *Desert Solitaire*. The book is a magnificent tribute to one of the most beautiful regions in America. Abbey worked in then-Arches National Monument as a seasonal ranger for three summers in the 1950s. His book, now required reading in many college English classes, chronicles one year, from April to September, in the park. He was at that time the only ranger assigned to Arches, and performed all of the services, from natural history interpretation to trash collecting, now attended to by a squadron of workers. *Desert Solitaire* is a love letter to the arches and arroyos, rocks and ridges, coyotes and cactus.

Yellow blossoms of prickly pear cactus,
Arches National Park, Utah

The man's passion for the desert was pure and unwavering. Upon his death in 1989 he was buried, Indian-style, under a pile of rocks at some undisclosed location in the hinterlands. You will find Abbey's masterpiece for sale in the parks' visitor's centers — I cannot recommend it too highly.

Enough on Abbey. Your experience of this part of the painted desert will probably begin in Moab, Utah and continue up the road into Arches National Park. You may want to avoid visiting the park around spring break or Easter time. Don't ask me how I know that, I just do. Another time to possibly avoid is around Labor Day, when the Colorado plateau country begins to cool off and city folk become restless. In mid-summer the park can become uncomfortably hot, and in the winter be prepared for snow and cold. But at either of those times, you will at least have much of the country to yourself.

The world's largest concentration of natural stone arches are found in Arches, and they are much in evidence along the 40-mile round-trip, paved road that leads deeply into the park. The road — at times bumper to bumper — is one of the most beautiful in the country, and leads visitors to such marvels as "South Park Avenue" where vertical slabs or fins of red Entrada sandstone resemble New York skyscrapers; the panoramic La Sal Mountain overlook; Courthouse Towers (collapsed fins now standing as

The dramatic canyon country of Capitol Reef National Park, Utah

Hoodoos — weathered rock pinnacles — predominate in Bryce Canyon National Park, Utah

isolated posts); Petrified Dunes; Balanced Rock; Double Arch; Pothole Arch; Delicate Arch; Sand Dune Arch; Skyline Arch; Devils Garden; and Landscape Arch (a 306-foot natural span).

There are many fine hiking trails in Arches, and it is always nice to get off the congested road and into the backcountry, even if it can be as crowded there. One of the most popular trails is the 3-mile round-trip walk to the exquisite Delicate Arch, in which the distant snowy La Sal Mountains are framed. If I had a dollar for every photograph that has ever been taken of Delicate Arch, I could buy country estates for all my friends and relatives. Near the trailhead are the remains of the Wolfe Ranch. Ohio native John Wesley Wolfe, a Civil War veteran, and his son moved to the remote valley in the late nineteenth century. All that remains today are several decaying buildings infested with mice and the remnants of a corral. Notice the tamarisk growing nearby — tamarisk was brought into the country from the Middle East in the 1920s and now makes itself a nuisance everywhere. A clear running stream nearby supports birdlife, snakes and frogs, the tadpoles of which can be seen in abundance throughout the shallows. Deer and coyote tracks tell us something about the night life.

While hiking in Arches and Canyonlands, try to stay on the trails so as not to destroy the soil. What? Not destroy the soil by walking on it? That's right. Soils in this unique area form a fragile black crust, dominated by cyanobacteria, which in places comprises over 70 percent of the living ground cover. These bacteria-bound top layers are surprisingly resistant to erosion in an area without sufficient rainfall to support a sod or grass cov-

The Colorado River en route to the Grand Canyon, Glen Canyon National Recreation Area, Utah

GETTING THERE

From Grand Junction take Interstate 70 west about 50 miles to the Cisco exit in Utah. Drive south here on State Route 128 (beautiful view of Fisher Towers on the Colorado River). The road ends at U.S. 191 just north of Moab. Take a right, heading north, to access **Arches National Park.** Take a left, heading south, to access **Canyonlands National Park.** The access road to the **Needles District** is 56 miles south of Moab. The road is on the west side of U.S. 191.

ering. Stepping off the trail, you destroy these important microbial communities and expose the ground to the invasive forces of wind and water erosion. In both Arches and Canyonlands it is often possible, and highly desirable, to walk on exposed rock surfaces instead of the fragile cryptobiotic soil.

Two of the great western rivers — the Green and the Colorado — make their confluence in Canyonlands National Park, my favorite park in the Painted Desert. Why? It is not nearly as crowded as Arches, and it is a hiker's paradise, with thousands of bizarre rock formations, and hundreds of miles of excellent trails. The park is conventionally divided into three regions — The Needles, The Maze, and The Island in the Sky. The Needles consists of the country south of the Colorado River, Island in the Sky lies north of the confluence, and The Maze is found west of the Green and Colorado.

The last, The Maze, is the least accessible and least visited of the three, with the end of the road — Hans Flat — 133 miles south and west of Moab (and Hans Flat is still miles from The Maze). This is truly wild country, and can be entered only by those with a four-wheel-drive vehicle, plenty of drinking water and a good pair of hiking boots. Prior to the park's formation in 1964, much of the country in The Maze had been essentially unexplored. Today, though, many desert rats are familiar with the features of this starkly beautiful Land of Standing Rocks. For those without four-wheel-drives, private tour companies in Moab can take you there, for a fee.

The Great White Throne near the Virgin River, Zion National Park, Utah

From Island in the Sky you have many fine overlooks with spectacular views. First, and often overlooked, is the scene at your feet. Many people ignore this one, but it is on this community that everything else is built. There are weathered chunks of reddish-brown sandstone, crusted bits of cryptobiotic soil, plants such as sage, prickly pear cactus, claret cup cactus, pinyon pine and juniper, the fallen feathers of raven and hawk, the scat of an owl, the bones of a mouse. Next there is the view 1,000 feet below the rim — the depths of the muddy Green and Colorado rivers, the rivers showing a jungle green along the banks. At a further distance are canyons, and canyons, and canyons. Finally, distant mountains on the horizon are more than 100 miles away. Island in the Sky is a place to stop awhile, and look, and think. No one can come away from the rim of Island in the Sky without having been humbled. Here is a scene that was already ancient when our ancestors were learning about arrowheads in Olduvai Gorge, and will still be there when our descendants are building starships to take them out into the galaxy.

The Needles region offers some of the best hiking in the park. The rangers at the Visitor's Center near the end of the road can supply an almost endless list of suggestions. One of my favorites is the trail to Angel Arch, which follows Salt Creek south from Peekaboo Spring. Another fine trail runs south from Paul Bunyan's Potty through Horse Canyon to Fortress Arch. To the west, the country is criss-crossed with trails to such features as Devil's Kitchen, Butler Flat, and Druid Arch. There are literally hundreds of prehistoric Indian sites in the Needles country — remember to take only pictures.

ROCKS THE COLOR OF FIRE: BRYCE CANYON NATIONAL PARK, CEDAR BREAKS NATIONAL MONUMENT AND CAPITOL REEF NATIONAL PARK

... a beautiful desolation.
—Ansel Adams

Hoodoos. That's the evocative word used to describe the eerie orange and red pinnacle formations that make Bryce Canyon National Park famous around the world. And the park is very well known. At the over-look to Bryce Canyon you will hear more languages than at a meeting of the United Nations — busloads of international tourists are driven in from Las Vegas nearly every day. In fact, each year over 1.5 million pilgrims journey to Bryce. And why not? Where else in the world can you see so many oddly shaped and brightly colored rock pillars, the distinctive hoodoos scattered over the countryside in sharp warrior-like ridges, solitary hermit spires, or closely-clustered familial groups. Even in early days the place was highly regarded. President Warren G. Harding set the area aside as Bryce Canyon National Monument in 1924. It was made a park in 1928, years before such parks as Arches and Canyonlands.

Though most people leave their cars only long enough to admire the view and snap a few pictures (which is fine and also beneficial to the back-country), there are some fantastic trails in Bryce Canyon. The Riggs Spring Loop, which runs to Riggs Spring via Mutton Hollow and then back via Yovimpa Pass, provides an excellent walkabout, as does the Under-the-Rim Trail. As the name suggests, the latter trail runs beneath the Pink Cliffs and can be taken for a short day hike, or a much longer excursion. Similarly, the Rim Trail leads from Bryce Point to Fairyland Point, and can be followed for its duration or for a short jaunt. Although Bryce Canyon is not, strictly speaking, desert country, it is an intrinsic part of the Painted Desert, and no trip (or book) on the region would be complete without its inclusion.

Similary, Cedar Breaks and Capitol Reef provide a desert experience in an upland environment. Cedar Breaks is a miniature version of Bryce Canyon, and there are many who believe its intense colors exceed those of Bryce Canyon. The red-and-orange-colored hoodoos of Cedar Breaks are situated in an immense coliseum that drops nearly 2,000 feet to its floor. As with Bryce Canyon, there are well-maintained trails all around the rim. The area, like the Grand Canyon, is popular with cross-country skiers in the winter months. The pink, yellow, orange and red rocks provide a striking contrast with the white snow, green pines and blue sky.

Capitol Reef, on the other hand, is not so much a hoodoo country as it is a wilderness of unusual sandstone formations and cliffs similar in places to Zion National Park. The area is noted for its enormous light-colored domes that evoke capitol buildings, and for its deep red-rock canyons and cliffs. The park is set along Waterpocket Fold, a wave of colorful rocks that extend along a 150-mile front. The colossal formation has been cut into various domes, gorges and cliffs by millions of years of erosion, all to the delight of photographers, artists, and hikers. In places, the desert varnish, sandstone crossbedding, and ages of erosion have created canyon walls with features similar to those found in artistic bas-reliefs. Ancient rock drawings are sometimes found on these walls. The park has few roads, other than the state road through the Fremont River gorge, and, with over a quarter of a million acres, is consequently an excellent place for hiking.

GETTING THERE

Bryce Canyon is accessed via U.S. 89. Sixty miles north of the Arizona state line, turn east on State Route 12 for 14 miles to the junction with the park road. Turn south on the park road, which accesses the west rim. The route to **Cedar Breaks** follows U.S. 89 for 41 miles north of the Arizona state line. Turn west on State Route 14. Twenty-six miles down the road is the access road to Cedar Breaks. Turn north and follow a few miles to the monument. **Capitol Reef** is best reached from Interstate 70 in south-central Utah. Leave the Interstate at Exit 147 and drive south on State Route 24 for around 70 miles to the park entrance. There is no gate for fee collection (as of 1996), and the road continues for around 10 miles through the park, with numerous turnouts and panoramic view points en route.

CATHEDRAL OF SILENCE:
ZION NATIONAL PARK

Nothing can exceed the wondrous beauty of Zion ... in the nobility
and beauty of the sculptures there is no comparison.
— Clarence Dutton, 1880

Such wonders as The Great White Throne, the Court of the Patriarchs,
and the Towers of the Virgin made Zion National Park a favorite of photographer Ansel Adams. Zion is, indeeed, a photographer's dream come true, with
sheer canyon walls of unbelievable height, time-scarred white rock domes,
cross-bedded sandstone formations, weirdly eroded slickrock, plunging waterfalls, hanging gardens of yellow columbine and green fern, and peaceful cottonwood groves that turn a brilliant yellow in the autumn. Much of the park
consists of a forested plateau deeply incised with the tributaries of ancient
watercourses, such as the North and East Forks of the Virgin River. Desert
and semi-desert vegetation prevails at lower elevations, with big-leafed sage
and prickly pear cactus flats,
and tangled patches of fox-
tail barley and Gambel oak.

Ninety percent of all
visitors confine their activities to the road at the bottom of Zion Canyon, but
there is another, larger park
accessible by a system of
excellent hiking trails. Two

GETTING THERE

Zion National Park: Twelve
miles north of St. George,
Utah exit Interstate 15 and
turn east on State Route 9.
Follow this road for 29 miles
to the park entrance, just east
of Virgin, Utah.

*Waterfall in the canyon of the Virgin River, Zion National
Park, Utah*

Petrified wood, Grand Canyon National Park, Arizona

of the best trails are the East Rim Trail, which leads from the East Entrance north past the White Cliffs and Stave Spring to Echo Canyon, and the West Rim Trail, which proceeds north over Horse Pasture Plateau to Lava Point. For any hiking in the backcountry, be certain to pack the appropriate USGS topographical maps. Rangers suggest that anyone having acrophobia — a fear of heights — avoid the West Rim Trail below West Rim Spring, Observation Point, Hidden Canyon, and the Canyon Overlook Trail. This may seem like an unnecessary admonition, but it is not. People fall to their deaths in these desert parks (particularly Grand Canyon).

OF TIME AND THE RIVER: GRAND CANYON NATIONAL PARK AND GLEN CANYON NATIONAL RECREATION AREA

In a dry, hot, monotonous forested plateau, seemingly boundless, you come suddenly and without warning upon the abrupt edge of a gigantic sunken landscape of the wildest, most multitudinous features ... [a] gloriously colored mountain-range countersunk in a level gray plain. It is a hard job to sketch it even in scrawniest outline; and, try as I may, not in the least sparing myself, I cannot tell the hundredth part of the wonders of its features.

— John Muir, *The Grand Canyon of the Colorado*

Sunset with contrails and pinyon pine, Grand Canyon National Park, Arizona

Immensity. That is the word that best describes the Grand Canyon. An immensity that momentarily stilled even the practiced pen of John Muir, who had so eloquently descibed everything from the giant sequoias of Yosemite to the floating glaciers of Glacier Bay. In the Grand Canyon the Colorado River has cut through the accumulated layers of the earth's surface

View of the Grand Canyon from the North Rim, looking west (Arizona)

Claret cup cactus on the rim of the Grand Canyon (Arizona)

to reach what Norman Maclean called the basement of time. In the vast, forlorn, twisting barranca the crust of the earth has been laid bare, so that we can peer deep inside the planet. A billion years of history can be seen in a glance, from Precambrian bedrock at the distant river's edge to fossilized sand dunes only a million years old at the rim. The view at either extreme, bottom or top, is staggering. Imagine gazing up at a building that towers with terraces and alcoves, walls and buttresses, hanging gardens and waterfalls, caves and seeps, ridges and side ridges, minor peaks and side canyons, bowls and amphitheaters more than one mile in the air. That is the approximate view from the bottom of the Grand Canyon. Now picture, as Muir suggests, a whole mountain range — the Front Range of Colorado, for example — turned upside down and sunk into the earth. Picture that scene painted in gaudy bright bands with all the colors of the rainbow — reds, greens, oranges, yellows, purples — and then lay the whole scene out beneath the immense blue Arizona sky, and you can understand why even the normally verbose Theodore Roosevelt was stunned into silence when he first stepped to the edge. Walking away from the rim, the man now carved in stone at Mt. Rushmore said, "The ages made it. Leave it alone."

GETTING THERE

The **South Rim** is located about 81 miles north of Flagstaff, Arizona via U.S. 180. The **North Rim** is more difficult to access. From Flagstaff drive north on U.S. 89 for 178 miles to Jacob Lake. Turn south on State Route 67 and follow it for 45 miles south to the Visitor's Center. State Route 67 is closed because of snow from autumn (date varies) to spring (usually open by around May 15th each year). **Glen Canyon** is accessed via Page, Arizona. Essentially everything just to the north of Page (Lake Powell and its environs) comprises the Glen Canyon National Recreation Area. There are places to rent boats and hire tour planes in Page — signs everywhere and every motel and hotel is well stocked with brochures for local tour operators.

There are two Grand Canyons — the South Rim and the North Rim. Although less than a dozen miles apart as the crow flies, they are distinctly different. The North Rim, a thousand feet higher than the South Rim and more remote from major interstates and towns, is less crowded (although crowded is a relative term here). The South Rim, with an elevation of 7,000 feet and direct access on U.S. 180 from Interstate 40 and Flagstaff, can be a congested place, especially during the tourist season, which, increasingly, corresponds with most of the snow-free months. About nine out of ten park visitors visit the South Rim, partly because the views there are thought to be better than those at the North Rim.

Trails are in abundance in the canyon, but

The Grand Canyon near Bright Angel (Arizona)

again the crowd situation (which will only get worse) means that you must make reservations by phone months in advance. Some people avoid this problem by taking extended day hikes, covering anywhere from 12 to 20 miles with a fraction of the load and discomfort of backpackers. This can be a good solution, but in either case carry, and drink, plenty of water. Not long ago my 35-year-old younger brother went backpacking in the Grand Canyon and collapsed from heat exhaustion brought on by exposure. He had failed to drink sufficient water on a sunny June day when the temperatures exceeded 100 degrees. A quick-thinking companion, a passing ranger, and an emergency IV saved him from who knows what. Treat the desert heat with respect — people have done more than collapse from the heat.

The two most popular trails are the Kaibab and Bright Angel trails. On both hikers must contend with mule trails, which can be rather disconcerting on a narrow path above a sheer drop-off. The trails, which begin at the South Rim and North Rim respectively, lead to the only bridge across the Colorado in the park, and to the popular Phantom Ranch area. Elsewhere in the park, there are hundreds of miles of trails on which you can find more solitude than on these two wilderness thoroughfares. Consult rangers about trails that are being maintained in this era of budget cuts.

View of the desolate backcountry of Canyonlands National Park (Utah)

A must-read book on the subject of Grand Canyon hiking is Colin
Fletcher's *The Man Who Walked Through Time*. Fletcher navigated the
entire length of the Grand Canyon in one long and sometimes harrowing
hike. Another great read is Edward Abbey's essay "Havasu" (in *Desert
Solitaire*), which describes five weeks spent by the author in the depths of
the Grand Canyon. And of course every Canyon-lover should own a copy
of Van Dyke's book *The Grand Canyon of the Colorado*, which, though
written a long time ago, is proving itself to be an immortal classic. The
Grand Canyon — like the Serengeti plains of Tanzania, the lake country of
England, the frozen peaks of Nepal — has inspired a whole library of
books, all written in tribute to one of nature's great creations.

In 1963, believe it or not, there was a plan by the Bureau of Reclama-
tion to dam the Grand Canyon at Bridge Canyon and Marble Canyon. If
the plan had been implemented, 90 percent of the water flow in the
national park would have been diverted through an immense tunnel drilled

under the Kaibab Plateau. At the same time, there was a plan to dam the Green River at Echo Park in Dinosaur National Park and to dam the Colorado River at a place called Glen Canyon, which is to the north of Grand Canyon National Park. Of the three projects, only the Glen Canyon dam was constructed. As a result, a region of spectacular natural beauty — more than 100 river miles of colorful gorges, arches, reefs, cliffs, slickrocks, spires, domes and ancient Indian ruins — was drowned beneath hundreds of feet of rapidly evaporating water. Today, the Glen Canyon Recreation Area (1,226,880 acres) surrounds the second largest resevoir in North America with 1,960 miles of shoreline. It is popular with houseboaters and bass fishermen. Both Natural Bridges National Monument and Rainbow Bridge National Monument, in the Glen Canyon country, provide a sense of what this area was like prior to damming.

Anyone interested in Glen Canyon before the dam should read Edward Abbey's essay "Down the River" (in *Desert Solitaire*). Abbey and his friend Ralph Newcomb were among the last rafters to float the Colorado River in Glen Canyon before the dam was constructed. Abbey wrote:

I was one of the lucky few ... who saw Glen Canyon before it was drowned. In fact I saw only a part of it but enough to real-ize that here was an Eden, a portion of the earth's original par-adise. To grasp the nature of the crime that was committed imagine the Taj Mahal or Chartres Cathedral buried in mud until only the spires remain visible.

SHE WORE A YELLOW RIBBON: MONUMENT VALLEY NAVAJO TRIBAL PARK AND CANYON DE CHELLY NATIONAL MONUMENT

We have had a spectacular and dangerous trip. All went well through Death Valley, Boulder Dam, Zion, North Rim, South Rim. Then we spent the night on Walpi Mesa, proceeded to Chinley, and had two spectacular, stormy days at Canyon de Chelly. I photographed the White House Ruins from almost the identical spot and time of the O'Sullivan picture! Can't wait until I see what I got.

—Ansel Adams,
letter to Beaumont and Nancy Newhall,
October 26, 1941

GETTING THERE

Monument Valley is basically everything north of
Kayenta, Arizona on either
side of U.S. 163, and extend-
ing slightly into southern
Utah. About 24 miles north of
Kayenta is the road to the
Visitor Center (turn east on
the well-marked road).
Guides can be hired and
more extensive back-country
tours arranged here. **Canyon
de Chelly** is located east of
Chinle, Arizona. Chinle is on
U.S. 191 about midway be-
tween Interstate 40 and the
Utah state line (191 runs
north and south). The access
road is in the middle of
Chinle, and is very well
marked. Turn east and follow
it to the Visitor's Center a few
miles further on.

In the heart of the Navajo country is one
of the most remarkable features in the
American West: Monument Valley. So inspir-
ing is the desert scenery here that six-time
Oscar winner John Ford used the valley,
exclusively, for his finest Western films,
including the cavalry trilogy *Fort Apache, She
Wore a Yellow Ribbon,* and *Rio Grande,* and
the masterpiece *Wagon Master* about the early
Mormons. In the park are dramatic monoliths, reddish sand dunes, traditional Navajo
hogans, and sheer crimson cliffs. The valley is
always changing, depending on the position
of the sun and moon and clouds. It is a place
that has challenged artists and photographers
for over a century, and is as starkly beautiful
at midday, with the isolated monoliths glow-
ing red beneath the sun, as at midnight, with
the same formations a luminous ghostly gray
beneath the stars.

Several hours to the south, near Chinle,
Arizona, is Canyon de Chelly National
Monument, which preserves the 1000-year-
old ruins of Pueblo cliff dwellers. The most
famous — the White House Ruins — have
to be seen to be believed, set as they are in a
dramatic and fantastically weathered sheer cliff. The first photographer to
visit the area was Timothy O'Sullivan, who accompanied the Wheeler government expedition in 1867, and exposed negatives that, as Ansel Adams
intimates in the epigraph, set the standard for all future photographers.
There are actually two canyons in the park — Canyon de Chelly (26
miles long) and Canyon del Muerto (25 miles long). Both are characterized by sheer red sandstone walls, ancient rock houses, and quiet groves of
cottonwoods. As with Monument Valley, licensed Navajo Indian guides
accompany all visitors on hikes and tours through the park. The White
House Ruins are the only ruins to which people can hike without hiring a
guide (a 3-mile round-trip, highly recommended but *very* steep if there are
health concerns).

Canyon de Chelly National Monument, Arizona, from the Wheeler Expedition.   *Photo courtesy of U.S.G.S.*

OTHER SITES

DEAD HORSE POINT STATE PARK — The park is named for the wild mustangs once herded here and tragically left to die. This site, located west of Moab via U.S. 191 and Highway 313, offers panoramic views of the canyon country. Dead Horse Point State Park, PO Box 609, Moab 84532 (801-259-2614).

ESCALANTE STATE PARK — An excellent nature trail here leads through a pinyon-juniper woodland where there are numerous fossilized trees. Escalante State Park, Escalante, Utah 84701 (801-826-4466)

HOVENWEEP NATIONAL MONUMENT — Hovenweep consists of a series of stone towers and cliff dwellings scattered in six distinct groups across extreme southeastern Utah and southwestern Colorado. It is best to get directions and a good map before setting out in search of these ruins. For more information contact Mesa Verde National Park.

KODACHROME STATE PARK — Kodachrome Basin, as the name implies, offers an incredible spectacle of bizarre sandstone formations, all changing depending on the position of the sun and the time of the year. Kodachrome Basin State Park, PO Box 238, Cannonville, Utah 84718.

MESA VERDE NATIONAL PARK — One of the crown jewel parks of the Southwest, Mesa Verde preserves an extensive series of cliff dwellings, including the remarkable Cliff Palace, Far View Ruins, Fewkes Canyon Ruins, Sun Temple, and Square Tower House. In places, the density of sites is over 100 per square mile. Excellent hiking trails are found in this park. Mesa Verde National Park, Colorado 81330 (303-529-4421/4543/4475)

NEWSPAPER ROCK STATE PARK — Newspaper Rock is an extensively marked rock panel located northwest of Monticello, Utah on Highway 211, the major access road to the Needles district of Canyonlands National Park. The petroglyphs here, which range from human hand prints to other more creative designs, are a must-see for anyone travelling into this portion of the Canyon Country.

FURTHER INFORMATION

Arches National Park
Box 907
Moab, Utah 84532
801-259-8161

Bryce Canyon National Park
Bryce Canyon, Utah 84717
801-834-5322

Bureau of Land Management
San Juan Resource Area
435 North Main
PO Box 7
Monticello, Utah 84535
801-587-2141

Grand Canyon National Park
PO Box 129
Grand Canyon, Arizona 86023
For South Rim lodging reservations call 520-638-2401. For North Rim lodging reservations call 801-586-7686. For camping reservations call 1-800-365-2267. For backpacking permit reservations call 520-526-0924.

Monument Valley Navajo Tribal Park
Kayenta, Arizona 86501
520-871-7371/6659

Natural Bridges National Monument
PO Box 1
Lake Powell, Utah 84533
801-259-5174

Canyon De Chelly National
  Monument
Box 588
Chinle, Arizona, 86503
602-674-5436

Canyonlands National Park
Moab, Utah 84532
801-259-7164

Canyonlands Natural History
  Association
30 South 100 East
Moab, Utah, 84532
801-259-6003

Capitol Reef National Park
Torrey, Utah 84775
801-425-3791

Cedar Breaks National
  Monument
82 North 100 East, Room 3
Cedar City, Utah 84720
801-586-9451

Glen Canyon National
  Recreation Area
Box 1507
Page, Arizona 86040
520-645-8200

Petrified Forest National Park
PO Box 2217
Petrified Forest National Park,
  Arizona 86028
520-524-6228

Rainbow Bridge National Monument
Glen Canyon National Recreation Area
Box 1507
Page, Arizona 86040
520-645-2511

Zion National Park
Springdale, Utah 84767
801-772-3256

Afterword

I really only want to say that we may love a place
and still be dangerous to it.
— Wallace Stegner,
"Thoughts on a Dry Land" from
The American West as Living Space

SO THERE YOU HAVE IT. A brief factual sketch of the deserts. With a bit of more lyrical prose scattered here and there, like patches of yellow brittle-bush, to enliven the more arid guidebook rhetoric. Having finished the text, allow me a few paragraphs, not of human or natural history but of practical philosophy, even politics. As you venture forth into the cactus country, dear friends, consider these few final thoughts. The desert lands are vast and ancient, but they are not invulnerable. They will outlast our civilization, but the effects of our impetuosity will also endure. Future generations will have to contend with radioactive soils and plants; with marginal grasslands turned into unproductive wastelands; with rivers dammed and diverted with little regard for downstream channels; with cities that were allowed to grow with all the logic of a tumor; with gaping holes left unfilled from open pit mining; with artifacts stolen not from ruins but from history; with species such as the condor, wolf, or jaguar confined to the corners and closets of state museums. To say nothing of our legacy on the reservations. At times I am reminded of the lines from Jeremiah: "And I brought you into a plentiful country, to eat the fruit therof and the goodness therof; but when ye entered, ye defiled my land, and made mine heritage an abomination." At other times I am less severe, not being so much of a sentimentalist as to paint an entirely benign picture of the Southwest prior to the arrival of the ox-drawn wagon.

But the basic point is this.

The desert needs
your help. As much as
you can give. And there
are some very easy, prac-
tical things that can be
done. The first involves
education — letting
other people know
where you work, live
and worship that you
care about these areas,
and that you want them
to care. This can be as
simple as having a spir-

Sunset, Joshua Tree National Park, Mojave Desert (California)

ited conversation at the bus stop, or writing a letter to your local paper or
legislator, or putting a bumper sticker on the back of the car. Sometimes it
can entail more of a commitment, such as preparing a slide show to share
with your children's class, or organizing the appearance of a guest speaker at
the local library or, in extreme cases, even writing an article or a book. The
second point is a corollary of the first and that is to participate, if only
through membership, in those organizations that are fighting for the deserts,
groups such as the Nature Conservancy, Wilderness Society, National
Audubon Society, Defenders of Wildlife, National Wildlife Federation,
World Wildlife Fund, and Sierra Club. In each case, your annual dues and
donations go far to helping the deserts, whose residents have no voice in
human forums but those among us who speak out for them. The last thing is
the most important in a democracy and that is to vote your values. The wildlands are living repositories of freedom, and that freedom is best protected, as
a first line of defense, by the man or woman who walks into a curtained
booth and pulls a voting lever.

There is so much more. Two last, but not minor, concerns. The first is
the Sagebrush Rebellion, which involves the sometimes militant efforts of
western idealogues to nullify federal ownership of public lands, including
desert lands. This is not a movement to be underestimated. We fought a
Civil War over the issue of state's rights, which is what energizes the
Sagebrush Rebellion, and that earlier conflict left 500,000 casualties on bat-
tlefields from Gettysburg, Pennsylvania to Glorieta Pass, New Mexico. The
Sagebrush Rebellion — and it is appropriately named — should be defused
now, before it gains momentum. What to do? Support federal law enforce-
ment and the rule of law, as well as those members of Congress who actively

oppose plans to sell public lands out-
right, transfer federal lands to state
ownership, or close national parks
such as Hovenweep in Utah (as a
means of preparing them to be sold).

The second concern is the growing American population and its
effect on the national parks. Anyone
who has been to Organ Pipe or
Joshua Tree in March knows what I
am talking about. The solution is
increase funds for park maintenance,
interpertation and operations, to
increase park personnel, to establish
new campgrounds and trails where
necessary, and in some cases to designate new parks. Some have argued,
in an era of fiscal conservatism, that
any measures beyond a rudimentary

*Prickly pear cactus, Grand Canyon National
Park, Arizona*

kind of institutional survival are folly. That is a defeatist position, and, with
regards to the Congress, a self-fulfilling prophecy. The American people love
their deserts a lot more than they do pork barrel fiascos or foreign aid fol-
lies. Above all, we need for the park concessionaires to return a fair amount
of their profits to that respective park, and for those funds not to disappear
into the general account of the U.S. Treasury.

I say all this not to fashion another shrill jeremiad, to belabor the obvious or preach to the converted, but to inch a lever beneath that immoveable

*Red sandstone rock formation with rising moon,
Monument Valley, Arizona*

object — public opinion
— and move it a bit fur-
ther down the dusty
road we call human
progress. Words, after all,
have power. Books can
make a difference. A
writer, in the end, has an
obligation not only to
criticize, but also to pro-
pose, to tell the truth in
all of its unrefined com-
plexity, but also to pro-

View from Land's End, looking west to the San Gabriel Mountains, Joshua Tree National Park, Mojave Desert (California)

vide a basis for good cheer, a simple affirmation of life. The deserts have done much for me — even saved my life one or twice — and I owe them at least a book.

The desert is many things. It is a bristlecone pine in the Snake Range that was already 2000 years old when a restless young carpenter went for a month-long walk in the Judaean desert. It is a lechuguilla agave reaching for the stars from the sand and gravel of a dry wash in northern Chihuahua. It is a cactus wren singing the sun up from its nest of twigs and feathers at the top of a 50-foot saguaro. It is a Yuma puma drinking from a *tinajas* in the Growler Mountains. It is the roar of a flashflood down a West Texas arroyo, and the howling wind in the Nevada sagebrush, and the way a heavy Mojave mountain range is lifted on shimmering heat waves from the bonds of the earth. It is a community, a civilization, a place of legends and legerdemain, tragedies and comedies, axioms and anecdotes, losses and lessons. It is a definite place and yet has no specific boundaries, beginning and ending on a landscape that is both temporal and spatial, figurative as well as literal. It includes the crumbling ruins of those who have risen and fallen in the past, as well as the air-conditioned homes of those on whose graves the future will walk. Above all, the desert is a part of what Wallace Stegner called the geography of hope.

Further Reading

Abbey, Edward. *Abbey's Road.* New York: Dutton, 1979.

_____. *Cactus Country.* New York: Time-Life, 1973.

_____. *Beyond the Wall.* New York: Holt, Rinehart and Winston, 1984.

_____. *Desert Solitaire.* New York: McGraw-Hill, 1968.

_____. *One Life at a Time, Please.* New York: Henry Holt, 1988.

_____. *The Best of Edward Abbey.* San Francisco: Sierra Club, 1984.

_____. *The Journey Home: Some Words in Defense of the American West.* New York: Dutton, 1977.

_____. *Slickrock.* With photographs by Philip Hyde. San Francisco: Sierra Club, 1971.

Alcock, John. *Sonoran Desert Spring.* Tucson: University of Arizona Press, 1994.

Austin, Mary. *The Land of Little Rain.* Boston: Houghton Mifflin, 1913.

Bandelier, Fanny, trans. *The Journey of Alvar Nunez Cabeza de Vaca.* New York: Barnes, 1905.

Banham, Peter Reyner. *Scenes in America Deserta.* Salt Lake City: Gibbs M. Smith, 1982.

Bartlett, John Russell. *Personal Narrative of Explorations and Incidents... Connected with the U.S. and Mexican Boundary Commission.* New York: Appleton, 1854.

Bensen, Lyman. *The Cacti of Arizona.* Tucson: University of Arizona Press, 1974.

Bensen, Lyman and Robert A. Darrow. *The Trees and Shrubs of the Southwestern Deserts.* Tucson: University of Arizona Press, 1976.

Betzinez, Jason. *I Fought With Geronimo.* Lincoln: University of Nebraska Press, 1959.

Bourke, John Gregory. *An Apache Campaign in the Sierra Madre.* New York: Scribner's, 1886.

_____. *On the Border with Crook.* New York: Scribner's, 1891.

Bowden, Charles. *Blue Desert.* Tucson: University of Arizona Press, 1986.

_____. *Desierto.* New York: Norton, 1991.

_____. *Frog Mountain Blues.* Tucson: University of Arizona Press, 1987.

_____. *Killing the Hidden Waters: The Slow Destruction of Water Resources in the American Southwest.* Austin: University of Texas Press, 1977.

Corle, Edwin. *The Gila: River of the Southwest.* New York: Rinehart, 1951.

Cruse, Thomas. *Apache Days and After.* Lincoln: University of Nebraska Press, 1987.

Davis, Britton. *The Truth About Geronimo.* New Haven: Yale University Press, 1929.

Davis, Goode P., Junior and David E. Brown, editors. *Man and Wildlife in Arizona: The American Exploration Period, 1824 – 1865.* Phoenix: Arizona Game and Fish Department, 1982.

Dobie, J. Frank. *The Mustangs.* New York: Little Brown, 1952.

_____. *Tongues of the Monte.* Austin: University of Texas Press, 1980.

Dutton, Clarence. *Report on the Geology of the High Plateaus of Utah.* Washington, D.C.: U.S. Government, 1880

_____. *Tertiary History of the Grand Cañon District.* Washington, D.C.: U.S. Government, 1882; Layton, Utah: Peregrine Smith, 1977.

Findley, Rowe. *Great American Deserts.* Washington, D.C.: National Geographic Society, 1972.

Fletcher, Colin. *The Man Who Walked Through Time.* New York: Knopf, 1968.

Fradkin, Philip. *A River No More.* New York: Alfred A. Knopf, 1981.

Garret, Pat. *The Authentic Life of Billy the Kid.* 1882. Reprint, Norman: University of Oklahoma Press, 1954.

Gillet, James B. *Six Years with the Texas Rangers.* New Haven: Yale University Press, 1925.

Goin, Peter. *Nuclear Landscapes.* Baltimore: Johns Hopkins University Press, 1991.

Goeztmann, William H. *Exploration & Empire: The Explorer and the Scientist in the Winning of the American West.* New York: Norton, 1967.

_____. *The West of the Imagination.* New York: Norton, 1986.

Horgan, Paul. *Great River: The Rio Grande in North American History.* New York: Rinehart and Company, 1954.

Horn, Tom. *Life of Tom Horn: A Vindication.* Denver: Louthan, 1904.

Howard, Oliver O. *My Life and Experiences Among Our Hostile Indians.* Hartord: Worthington, 1907.

Humphrey, Robert R. *The Boojum and Its Home.* Tucson: University of Arizona Press, 1974.

Jaeger, Edmund C. *Desert Wild Flowers.* Stanford: Stanford University Press, 1964.

_____. *Desert Wildlife.* Stanford: Stanford University Press, 1961.

_____. *The California Deserts.* Stanford: Stanford University Press, 1965.

_____. *The North American Deserts.* Stanford: Stanford University Press, 1967.

Jett, Stephen J. *Navajo Wildlands.* With photographs by Philip Hyde. San Francisco: Sierra Club, 1967.

Krutch, Joseph. *The Desert Year.* New York: William Sloane, 1952; Viking, 1963.

_____. *The Forgotten Peninsula.* New York: William Sloane, 1961.

_____. *The Grand Canyon.* New York: William Sloane, 1958.

_____. *The Voice of the Desert.* New York: William Sloane, 1954.

Leopold, Aldo. *Round River.* New York: Oxford University Press, 1953.

Leopold, A. Starker. *The Desert.* New York: Time-Life, 1961.

_____. *Wildlife of Mexico: The Game Birds and Mammals.* Berkeley: University of California Press, 1957.

Lockwood, Frank C. *The Apache Indians.* Lincoln: University of Nebraska Press, 1987.

Lopez, Barry. *Desert Notes.* New York: Scribner's, 1976.

McNamee, Gregory. *The Gila River.* New York: Crown Publishing, 1992.

Miles, Elton. *Tales of the Big Bend.* College Station: Texas A & M University Press, 1976.

Miles, Nelson. *Personal Recollections and Observations.* New York: Werner, 1896.

Nabhan, Gary. *The Desert Smells Like Rain: A Naturalist in Papago Indian Country.* San Francisco: North Point, 1982.

_____. *Gathering the Desert.* Tucson: University of Arizona Press, 1985.

Oppelt, Norman T. *Guide to Prehistoric Ruins of the Southwest.* Boulder: Pruett Publishing, 1981.

Pattie, James O. *Personal Narrative.* Lincoln: University of Nebraska Press, 1982.

Peacock, Doug. *Baja.* New York: Henry Holt, 1992.

Powell, John Wesley. *The Exploration of the Colorado River.* Washington: U.S. Government, 1875; New York: Dover, 1961.

Reintroduction of the Mexican Wolf Within its Historic Range in the Southwestern United States. Draft Environmental Impact Statement. Fish and Wildlife Service. U.S. Department of the Interior. June, 1995. Region 2. Albuquerque, New Mexico.

Steinhart, Peter. *California's Wild Heritage: Threatened and Endangerd Animals in the Golden State.* San Francisco: Sierra Club, 1991.

Stegner, Wallace. *Beyond the Hundredth Meridian: John Wesley Powell and the Second Opening of the West.* Boston: Houghton Mifflin, 1954.

_____. *Clarence Dutton: An Appraisal.* Salt Lake City: University of Utah Press, 1936.

_____. *The American West as Living Space.* Ann Arbor: University of Michigan Press, 1987.

_____. *The Sound of Mountain Water.* Lincoln: University of Nebraska Press, 1985.

Thrapp, Daniel. *The Conquest of Apacheria.* Norman: University of Oklahoma Press, 1967.

Trimble, Stephen. *The Sagebrush Ocean: A Natural History of the Great Basin Desert.* Reno: University of Nevada Press, 1991.

Twain, Mark. *Roughing It.* New York: The Century Company, 1872.

Van Dyke, John Charles. *The Desert.* New York: Scribner's, 1901; Layton, Utah: Peregrine Smith, 1908.

_____. *The Grand Canyon of the Colorado.* New York: Scribner's, 1920.

Wellman, Paul I. *Death in the Desert: The Fifty Years' War for the Great Southwest.* Lincoln: University of Nebraska Press, 1987.

Williams, Terry Tempest. *Pieces of White Shell: A Journey to Navajoland.* New York: Scribner's, 1984.

_____. *Refuge.* New York: Pantheon, 1991.

Zwinger, Ann. *A Desert Country Near the Sea: A Natural History of the Cape Region of Baja California.* New York: Harper & Row, 1983.

_____. *Downcanyon.* Tucson: University of Arizona Press, 1995.

_____. *Run, River, Run.* New York: Harper & Row, 1975.

_____. *Wind in the Rock.* New York: Harper & Row, 1978.

Index

Books by John A. Murray

The Indian Peaks Wilderness

Wildlife in Peril: *The Endangered Mammals of Colorado*

The Gila Wilderness

The Last Grizzly, and Other Southwestern Bear Stories
(with David Brown)

The South San Juan Wilderness

A Republic of Rivers:
Three Centuries of Nature Writing from Alaska and the Yukon

The Islands and the Sea:
Five Centuries of Nature Writing from the Caribbean

The Great Bear: *Contemporary Writings on the Grizzly*

Nature's New Voices

Wild Hunters: *Predators in Peril*
(with Monte Hummel and Sherri Pettigrew)

Wild Africa: *Three Centuries of Nature Writing from Africa*

Out Among the Wolves: *Contemporary Writings on the Wolf*

A Thousand Leagues of Blue: *The Sierra Club Book of the Pacific*

American Nature Writing: *1994*

The Sierra Club Nature Writing Handbook

Grizzly Bears

American Nature Writing: *1995*

The Walker's Companion (with Dave Wallace and others)

American Nature Writing: *1996*

Alaska